THE KINGFISHER

THE
KINGFISHER

POEMS BY

AMY CLAMPITT

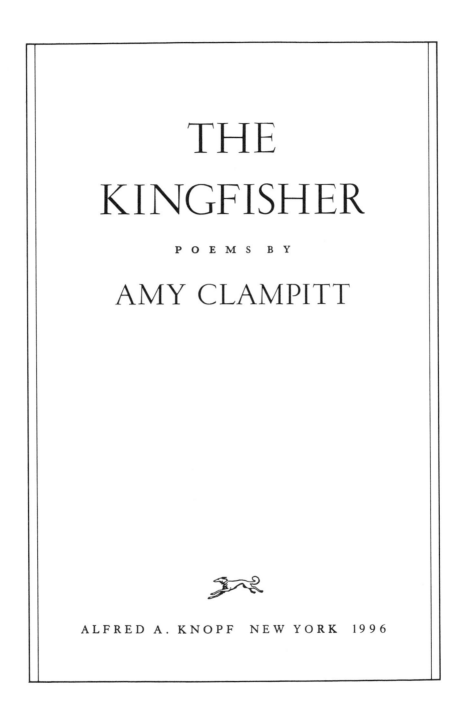

ALFRED A. KNOPF   NEW YORK   1996

THIS IS A BORZOI BOOK
PUBLISHED BY ALFRED A. KNOPF, INC.

ACKNOWLEDGMENTS

For their help with this book, the author wishes to record her thanks to Mary Jo Salter, Doris Myers, Linda Spencer, John Macrae III, Howard Moss, Frederick Turner, Brad Leithauser, Ann Close, Alice Quinn, and Harold Korn.

Grateful acknowledgment is made to the following periodicals, in which poems in this collection have previously appeared: *The Atlantic Monthly:* "The Cormorant in Its Element," "Fog," "On the Disadvantages of Central Heating," "Slow Motion"; *Chicago Review:* "Gradual Clearing"; *The Christian Science Monitor:* "Dancers Exercising," "The Edge of the Hurricane," "Remembering Greece," "Trasimene" (under the title "Umbrian Painters"); *The Kenyon Review:* "Imago," "Marginal Employment," "Or Consider Prometheus," "Rain at Bellagio," "Triptych"; *The Massachusetts Review:* "Amaranth and Moly; *The Nation:* "The Outer Bar"; *New England Review:* "A Procession at Candlemas"; *The New Republic:* "Beach Glass," "Marine Surface, Low Overcast"; *The New Yorker:* "Beethoven, Opus 111," "Camouflage," "The Cove," "Exmoor," "The Kingfisher," "Lindenbloom," "The Quarry," "Salvage," "The Smaller Orchid" (under the title "Ladies' Tresses"), "The Sun Underfoot Among the Sundews," "Tepoztlán," "Times Square Water Music"; *Poetry:* "Balms"; *Poetry Northwest:* "Sunday Music"; *Prairie Schooner:* "Botanical Nomenclature," "Meridian," "A Resumption, or Possibly a Remission," "The Woodlot"; and *The Yale Review:* "Letters from Jerusalem," "Stacking the Straw."

LIBRARY OF CONGRESS CATALOGING IN PUBLICATION DATA
Clampitt, Amy.
The kingfisher.
(Knopf poetry series; 9)
I. Title.
PS3553.L23K5   1982   811'.54   82–47963
ISBN 0–394–52840–9   AACR2
ISBN 0–394–71251–X (pbk.)

Manufactured in the United States of America
Published January 24, 1983
Reprinted Eight Times
Tenth Printing, April 1996

For Hal

As kingfishers catch fire, dragonflies draw flame . . .

—GERARD MANLEY HOPKINS

CONTENTS

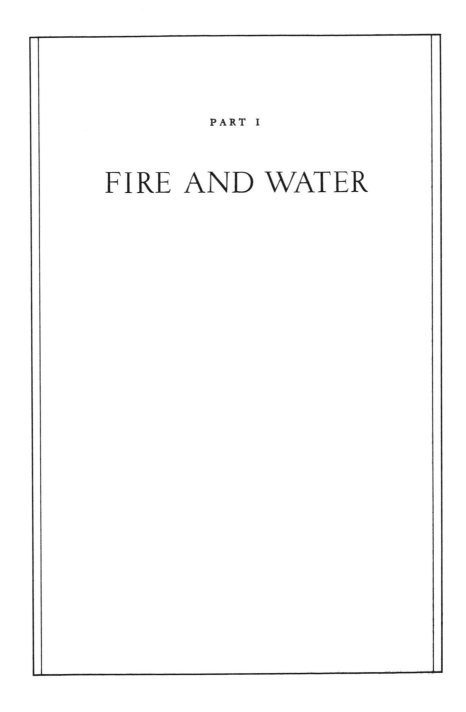

PART I

FIRE AND WATER

THE COVE

Inside the snug house, blue willow-ware
plates go round the dado, cross-stitch
domesticates the guest room, whole nutmegs
inhabit the spice rack, and when there's fog
or a gale we get a fire going, listen
to Mozart, read Marianne Moore, or
sit looking out at the eiders, trig
in their white-over-black as they tip
and tuck themselves into the swell, almost
as though diving under the eiderdown
in a *gemütlich* hotel room at Innsbruck.

At dusk we watch a porcupine, hoary
quadruped, emerge from under the spruce trees,
needle-tined paddle tail held out straight
behind, as though the ground were negotiable
only by climbing, to examine the premises,
and then withdraw from the (we presume)
alarming realm of the horizontal into
the up-and-down underbrush of normality.

From the sundeck, overhung by a gale-
hugged mountain ash, limbs blotched
and tufted with lichen, where in good
weather, every time we look up there's
a new kind of warbler flirting, all ombré
and fine stitchery, through the foliage,
one midday, looking down at the grass
we noticed a turtle—domed repoussé

3

leather with an underlip of crimson—
as it hove eastward, a covered
wagon intent on the wrong direction.

Where at low tide the rocks, like the
back of an old sheepdog or spaniel, are
rugg'd with wet seaweed, the cove
embays a pavement of ocean, at times
wrinkling like tinfoil, at others
all isinglass flakes, or sun-pounded
gritty glitter of mica; or hanging
intact, a curtain wall just frescoed
indigo, so immense a hue, a blue
of such majesty it can't be looked at,
at whose apex there pulses, even
in daylight, a lighthouse, light-
pierced like a needle's eye.

FOG

A vagueness comes over everything,
as though proving color and contour
alike dispensable: the lighthouse
extinct, the islands' spruce-tips
drunk up like milk in the
universal emulsion; houses
reverting into the lost
and forgotten; granite
subsumed, a rumor
in a mumble of ocean.
                        Tactile
definition, however, has not been
totally banished: hanging
tassel by tassel, panicled
foxtail and needlegrass,
dropseed, furred hawkweed,
and last season's rose-hips
are vested in silenced
chimes of the finest,
clearest sea-crystal.
                        Opacity
opens up rooms, a showcase
for the hueless moonflower
corolla, as Georgia
O'Keeffe might have seen it,
of foghorns; the nodding
campanula of bell buoys;
the ticking, linear
filigree of bird voices.

GRADUAL CLEARING

Late in the day the fog
wrung itself out like a sponge
in glades of rain,
sieving the half-invisible
cove with speartips;
then, in a lifting
of wisps and scarves, of smoke-rings
from about the islands, disclosing
what had been wavering
fishnet plissé as a smoothness
of peau-de-soie or just-ironed
percale, with a tatting
of foam out where the rocks are,
the sheened no-color of it,
the bandings of platinum
and magnesium suffusing,
minute by minute, with clandestine
rose and violet, with opaline
nuance of milkweed, a texture
not to be spoken of above a whisper,
began, all along the horizon,
gradually to unseal
like the lip of a cave
or of a cavernous,
single, pearl-
engendering seashell.

THE OUTER BAR

When through some lacuna, chink, or interstice
in the unlicensed free-for-all that goes
on without a halt out there all day, all night,
all through the winter,

one morning at low tide you walk dry-shod across
a shadow isthmus to the outer bar,
you find yourself, once over, sinking at every step
into a luscious mess—

a vegetation of unbarbered, virgin, foot-thick
velvet, the air you breathe an aromatic
thicket, odors in confusion starting up
at every step like partridges

or schools of fishes, an element you swim through
as to an unplanned, headily illicit
interview. The light out there, gashed
by the surf's scimitar,

is blinding, a rebuke—Go back! Go back!—
behind the silhouetted shipwreck (Whose?
When did it happen? Back in the village
nobody can tell you),

the bell buoy hunkering knee-deep in foam,
a blood-red-painted harbinger. How strange
a rim, back where you came from,
of familiar portents

reviewed from this *isola bella,* paradise
inside a prison rockpile—the unravished
protégé of guardians so lawless, refuge
moated up in such a shambles!

Your mind keeps turning back to look at them—
chain-gang archangels that in their prismatic
frenzy fall, gall and gash the daylight
out there, all through the winter.

SEA MOUSE

The orphanage of possibility
has had to be expanded to
admit the sea mouse. No one
had asked for such a thing,
or prophesied its advent,

sheltering under ruching
edges of sea lettuce—
a wet thing but pettable
as, seen in the distance,
the tops of copses,

sun-honeyed, needle-pelted
pine trees, bearded barley,
or anything newborn not bald
but furred. No rodent this
scabrous, this unlooked-for

foundling, no catnip plaything
for a cat to worry, not even
an echinoderm, the creature
seems to be a worm. Silk-spiny,
baby-mummy-swaddled, it's

at home where every corridor
is mop-and-bucket scrubbed
and aired from wall to wall
twice daily by the inde-
fatigable tidal head nurse.

BEACH GLASS

While you walk the water's edge,
turning over concepts
I can't envision, the honking buoy
serves notice that at any time
the wind may change,
the reef-bell clatters
its treble monotone, deaf as Cassandra
to any note but warning. The ocean,
cumbered by no business more urgent
than keeping open old accounts
that never balanced,
goes on shuffling its millenniums
of quartz, granite, and basalt.
                              It behaves
toward the permutations of novelty—
driftwood and shipwreck, last night's
beer cans, spilt oil, the coughed-up
residue of plastic—with random
impartiality, playing catch or tag
or touch-last like a terrier,
turning the same thing over and over,
over and over. For the ocean, nothing
is beneath consideration.
                              The houses
of so many mussels and periwinkles
have been abandoned here, it's hopeless
to know which to salvage. Instead
I keep a lookout for beach glass—
amber of Budweiser, chrysoprase

of Almadén and Gallo, lapis
by way of (no getting around it,
I'm afraid) Phillips'
Milk of Magnesia, with now and then a rare
translucent turquoise or blurred amethyst
of no known origin.
                    The process
goes on forever: they came from sand,
they go back to gravel,
along with the treasuries
of Murano, the buttressed
astonishments of Chartres,
which even now are readying
for being turned over and over as gravely
and gradually as an intellect
engaged in the hazardous
redefinition of structures
no one has yet looked at.

MARINE SURFACE,
LOW OVERCAST

Out of churned aureoles
this buttermilk, this
herringbone of albatross,
floss of mercury,
déshabille of spun
aluminum, furred with a velouté
of looking-glass,

a stuff so single
it might almost be lifted,
folded over, crawled underneath
or slid between, as nakedness-
caressing sheets, or donned
and worn, the train-borne
trapping of an unrepeatable
occasion,

this wind-silver
rumpling as of oatfields,
a suede of meadow,
a nub, a nap, a mane of lustre
lithe as the slide
of muscle in its
sheath of skin,

laminae of living tissue,
mysteries of flex,
affinities of texture,
subtleties of touch, of pressure

and release, the suppleness
of long and intimate
association,

new synchronies of fingertip,
of breath, of sequence,
entities that still can rouse,
can stir or solder,
whip to a froth, or force
to march in strictly
hierarchical formation

down galleries of sheen, of flux,
cathedral domes that seem to hover
overturned and shaken like a basin
to the noise of voices,
from a rustle to the jostle
of such rush-hour
conglomerations

no loom, no spinneret, no forge, no factor,
no process whatsoever, patent
applied or not applied for,
no five-year formula, no fabric
for which pure imagining,
except thus prompted,
can invent the equal.

THE SUN UNDERFOOT
AMONG THE SUNDEWS

An ingenuity too astonishing
to be quite fortuitous is
this bog full of sundews, sphagnum-
lined and shaped like a teacup.
                              A step
down and you're into it; a
wilderness swallows you up:
ankle-, then knee-, then midriff-
to-shoulder-deep in wetfooted
understory, an overhead
spruce-tamarack horizon hinting
you'll never get out of here.
                              But the sun
among the sundews, down there,
is so bright, an underfoot
webwork of carnivorous rubies,
a star-swarm thick as the gnats
they're set to catch, delectable
double-faced cockleburs, each
hair-tip a sticky mirror
afire with sunlight, a million
of them and again a million,
each mirror a trap set to
unhand unbelieving,

                              that either
a First Cause said once, "Let there
be sundews," and there were, or they've
made their way here unaided
other than by that backhand, round-
about refusal to assume responsibility
known as Natural Selection.
                              But the sun
underfoot is so dazzling
down there among the sundews,
there is so much light
in the cup that, looking,
you start to fall upward.

BOTANICAL
NOMENCLATURE

Down East people, not being botanists,
call it "that pink-and-blue flower
you find along the shore." Wildflower
guides, their minds elsewhere, mumble
"sea lungwort or oysterleaf" as a label
for these recumbent roundels, foliage
blued to a driftwood patina
growing outward, sometimes to the
size of a cathedral window,
stemrib grisaille edge-tasseled
with opening goblets, with bugles
in miniature, mauve through cerulean,
toggled into a seawall scree,
these tuffets of skyweed
neighbored by a climbing tideline,
by the holdfasts, the gargantuan lariats
of kelp, a landfall of seaweed:

Mertensia, the learned Latin
handle, proving the uses of taxonomy,
shifts everything abruptly inland,
childhoodward, to what we called then
(though not properly) bluebells:
spring-bottomland glades standing upright,
their lake-evoking sky color
a trapdoor, a window letting in distances
all the way to the ocean—
reaching out, *nolens volens,*
as one day everything breathing

will reach out, with just such
bells on its fingers, to touch
without yet quite having seen
the unlikelihood, the ramifying
happenstance, the mirroring
marryings of all likeness.

ON THE DISADVANTAGES
OF CENTRAL HEATING

cold nights on the farm, a sock-shod
stove-warmed flatiron slid under
the covers, mornings a damascene-
sealed bizarrerie of fernwork
    decades ago now

waking in northwest London, tea
brought up steaming, a Peak Frean
biscuit alongside to be nibbled
as blue gas leaps up singing
    decades ago now

damp sheets in Dorset, fog-hung
habitat of bronchitis, of long
hot soaks in the bathtub, of nothing
quite drying out till next summer:
    delicious to think of

hassocks pulled in close, toasting-
forks held to coal-glow, strong-minded
small boys and big eager sheepdogs
muscling in on bookish profundities
    now quite forgotten

the farmhouse long sold, old friends
dead or lost track of, what's salvaged
is this vivid diminuendo, unfogged
by mere affect, the perishing residue
    of pure sensation

MERIDIAN

First daylight on the bittersweet-hung
sleeping porch at high summer : dew
all over the lawn, sowing diamond-
point-highlighted shadows :
the hired man's shadow revolving
along the walk, a flash of milkpails
passing : no threat in sight, no hint
anywhere in the universe, of that

apathy at the meridian, the noon
of absolute boredom : flies
crooning black lullabies in the kitchen,
milk-soured crocks, cream separator
still unwashed : what is there to life
but chores and more chores, dishwater,
fatigue, unwanted children : nothing
to stir the longueur of afternoon

except possibly thunderheads :
climbing, livid, turreted alabaster
lit up from within by splendor and terror
—forked lightning's
                              split-second disaster.

A RESUMPTION,
OR POSSIBLY A REMISSION

for my sister Beth

Waking to all that white, as week by week
the inland ravines of a two-river city
filled up with it, was like the resumption
of a state of grace, as in dreams of being carried.
Nothing disturbed it: not the owl that came
rowing out at noon, soundless as fur,
nor the great horned ones' profundo
yelp from some outpost among oaks'
dun, nattering cling-leaves. In that
white habitat, the precarious architect
of ledges and cornices, of bridges
suspended with the ease of hammocks, even
those halloos came through as friendly.

Though on days of thaw a ponderous
icicle-fall, a more and more massively
glistening overhang, gave birth to daggers,
and though we'd hear our alcoholic landlord
(he came once beseeching the loan of
a bottle opener) being yelled at
by the spouse-in-charge, who would then
address herself to a parlor organ,
pumping out consolation with a vengeance,
from January nearly to the willowy
landfall of April, when new excitements
and misgivings began to intervene, to live
moated and immured inside the castle-keep
of all that white was to discover
even the Ur-nightmare of being
dropped, of waking up abandoned,
gone miraculously into remission.

I find I can no longer summon the layout
of that apartment. But the scene outside it
either reinvents, or subsumes uninterrupted,
a state that can't be gone back to: from
one window a pair of cardinals, she olive-
muted and red of beak, as though (you said)
she'd put on lipstick, he the scarlet-
suited royal mite of a Goya portrait,
meteors' scathing anomaly slowed down
and mollified to a quasi-domestic,
seed-eating familiar; next door
a silent house, walks uncleared week
after week, snowdrifts accumulating,
their tented pavilions overhung
by an old, crone-dark catalpa
metamorphosing, snowfall by snowfall,
into a hammock, the burden of all
that white, the deepening sag of it,
upheld as by a nursing mother.

A PROCESSION AT CANDLEMAS

I

Moving on or going back to where you came from,
bad news is what you mainly travel with:
a breakup or a breakdown, someone running off

or walking out, called up or called home:
death in the family. Nudged from their stanchions
outside the terminal, anonymous of purpose

as a flock of birds, the bison of the highway
funnel westward onto Route 80, mirroring
an entity that cannot look into itself and know

what makes it what it is. Sooner or later
every trek becomes a funeral procession.
The mother curtained in Intensive Care—

a scene the mind leaves blank, fleeing instead
toward scenes of transhumance, the belled sheep
moving up the Pyrenees, red-tasseled pack llamas

footing velvet-green precipices, the Kurdish
women, jingling with bangles, gorgeous
on their rug-piled mounts—already lying dead,

bereavement altering the moving lights
to a processional, a feast of Candlemas.
Change as child-bearing, birth as a kind

of shucking off: out of what began
as a Mosaic insult—such a loathing
of the common origin, even a virgin,

having given birth, needs purifying—
to carry fire as though it were a flower,
the terror and the loveliness entrusted

into naked hands, supposing God might have,
might actually need a mother: people have
at times found this a way of being happy.

A Candlemas of moving lights along Route 80;
lighted candles in a corridor from Arlington
over the Potomac, for every carried flame

the name of a dead soldier: an element
fragile as ego, frightening as parturition,
necessary and intractable as dreaming.

The lapped, wheelborne integument, layer
within layer, at the core a dream of
something precious, ripped: Where are we?

The sleepers groan, stir, rewrap themselves
about the self's imponderable substance,
or clamber down, numb-footed, half in a drowse

of freezing dark, through a Stonehenge
of fuel pumps, the bison hulks slantwise
beside them, drinking. What is real except

what's fabricated? The jellies glitter
cream-capped in the cafeteria showcase;
gumball globes, Life Savers cinctured

in parcel gilt, plop from their housings
perfect, like miracles. Comb, nail clipper,
lip rouge, mirrors and emollients embody,

niched into the washroom wall case,
the pristine seductiveness of money.
Absently, without inhabitants, this

nowhere oasis wears the place name
of Indian Meadows. The westward-trekking
transhumance, once only, of a people who,

in losing everything they had, lost even
the names they went by, stumbling past
like caribou, perhaps camped here. Who

can assign a trade-in value to that sorrow?
The monk in sheepskin over tucked-up saffron
intoning to a drum becomes the metronome

of one more straggle up Pennsylvania Avenue
in falling snow, a whirl of tenderly
remorseless corpuscles, street gangs

amok among magnolias' pregnant wands,
a stillness at the heart of so much whirling:
beyond the torn integument of childbirth,

sometimes, wrapped like a papoose into a grief
not merely of the ego, you rediscover almost
the rest-in-peace of the placental coracle.

2

Of what the dead were, living, one knows
so little as barely to recognize
the fabric of the backward-ramifying

antecedents, half-noted presences
in darkened rooms: the old, the feared,
the hallowed. Never the same river

drowns the unalterable doorsill. An effigy
in olive wood or pear wood, dank
with the sweat of age, walled in the dark

at Brauron, Argos, Samos: even the unwed
Athene, who had no mother, born—it's declared—
of some man's brain like every other pure idea,

had her own wizened cult object, kept
out of sight like the incontinent whimperer
in the backstairs bedroom, where no child

ever goes—to whom, year after year,
the fair linen of the sacred peplos
was brought in ceremonial procession—

flutes and stringed instruments, wildflower-
hung cattle, nubile Athenian girls, young men
praised for the beauty of their bodies. Who

can unpeel the layers of that seasonal
returning to the dark where memory fails,
as birds re-enter the ancestral flyway?

Daylight, snow falling, knotting of gears:
Chicago. Soot, the rotting backsides
of tenements, grimed trollshapes of ice

underneath the bridges, the tunnel heaving
like a birth canal. Disgorged, the infant
howling in the restroom; steam-table cereal,

pale coffee; wall-eyed TV receivers, armchairs
of molded plastic: the squalor of the day
resumed, the orphaned litter taken up again

unloved, the spawn of botched intentions,
grief a mere hardening of the gut,
a set piece of what can't be avoided:

parents by the tens of thousands living
unthanked, unpaid but in the sour coin
of resentment. Midmorning gray as zinc

along Route 80, corn-stubble quilting
the underside of snowdrifts, the cadaverous
belvedere of windmills, the sullen stare

of feedlot cattle; black creeks puncturing
white terrain, the frozen bottomland
a mush of willow tops; dragnetted in ice,

the Mississippi. Westward toward the dark,
the undertow of scenes come back to, fright
riddling the structures of interior history:

Where is it? Where, in the shucked-off
bundle, the hampered obscurity that has been
for centuries the mumbling lot of women,

did the thread of fire, too frail
ever to discover what it meant, to risk
even the taking of a shape, relinquish

the seed of possibility, unguessed-at
as a dream of something precious? Memory,
that exquisite blunderer, stumbling

like a migrant bird that finds the flyway
it hardly knew it knew except by instinct,
down the long-unentered nave of childhood,

late on a midwinter afternoon, alone
among the snow-hung hollows of the windbreak
on the far side of the orchard, encounters

sheltering among the evergreens, a small
stilled bird, its cap of clear yellow
slit by a thread of scarlet—the untouched

nucleus of fire, the lost connection
hallowing the wizened effigy, the mother
curtained in Intensive Care: a Candlemas

of moving lights along Route 80, at nightfall,
in falling snow, the stillness and the sorrow
of things moving back to where they came from.

THE DAKOTA

Grief for a generation—all
the lonely people
gone, the riffraff
out there now mainly pigeons—
steps from its limousine
and lights a taper
inside the brownstone catacomb
of the Dakota. Pick up
the wedding rice, take out
the face left over from
the funeral nobody came to,
bring flowers, leave them woven
with the lugubrious ironwork
of the Dakota. Grief
is original, but it
repeats itself: there's nothing
more original that it can do.

TIMES SQUARE
WATER MUSIC

By way of a leak
in the brickwork
beside a stairway
in the Times Square
subway, midway
between the IR
and the BM T, weeks
of sneaking seepage
had smuggled in,
that morning,
a centimeter
of standing water.

To ward off the herd
we tend to turn into,
turned loose on
the tiered terrain
of the Times Square
subway, somebody
had tried, with
a half-hearted
barricade or tether
of twine,
to cordon off
the stairway—

as though anyone
could tie up seepage
into a package—
down which the
water, a dripping
escapee, was surrep-
titiously proceeding
with the intent,
albeit inadvertent,
in time, at an
inferior level,
to make a lake.

Having gone round
the pond thus far
accumulated, bound
for the third, infra-
infernal hollow
of the underground,
where the N, RR,
and QB cars are
wont to travel,
in mid-descent I
stopped, abruptly way-
laid by a sound.

Alongside the iron-
runged nethermost
stairway, under
the banister,
a hurrying skein
of moisture had begun,
on its way down,
to unravel
into the trickle
of a musical
minuscule
waterfall.

Think of spleen-
wort, of moss
and maiden-
hair fernwork,
think of water
pipits, of ouzels
and wagtails
dipping into
the course of it
as the music
of it oozes
from the walls!

Think of it
undermining
the computer's
cheep, the time
clock's hiccup,
the tectonic
inchings of it
toward some
general crackup!
Think of it, think of
water running, running,
running till it
               falls!

PART II

AIRBORNE,
EARTHBOUND

THE EDGE
OF THE HURRICANE

Wheeling, the careening
winds arrive with lariats
and tambourines of rain.
Torn-to-pieces, mud-dark
flounces of Caribbean

cumulus keep passing,
keep passing.   By afternoon
rinsed transparencies begin
to open overhead, Mediterranean
windowpanes of clearness

crossed by young gusts'
vaporous fripperies, liquid
footprints flying, lacewing
leaf-shade brightening
and fading. Sibling

gales stand up on point
in twirling fouettés
of debris. The day ends
bright, cloud-wardrobe
packed away. Nightfall

hangs up a single moon
bleached white as laundry,
serving notice yet again how
levity can also trample,
drench, wring and mangle.

AMARANTH AND MOLY

The night we bailed out Jolene from Riker's Island
tumbleweeds in such multitudes were blowing through the dark
it might almost have been Wyoming. Built like a willow
or a John Held flapper, from the shoulders up
she was pure Nefertiti, and out of that divine
brown throat came honey and cockleburs.
She had nine children and no identifiable husband.
She wore a headcloth like a tiara above a sack dress
improvised from a beach towel. She'd turned larceny
against the bureaucracy into an art form.
When they raised the subway fare and simultaneously
cut back on Human Resources, Jolene
began jumping turnstiles as a matter of principle.
The police caught up with her at approximately
the fifteenth infraction, and the next thing
anybody knew, she'd been carted off
to the Women's House of D.
                              Now that it's
been shifted to the other side of the East River,
bailing anybody out becomes an all-night expedition—
a backhanded kind of joyride, comparable
to crossing the Styx or the Little Big Horn
in a secondhand Volkswagen. You enter a region
of landfill, hamburger loess, a necropolis
of coffee grounds, of desiccated *Amaranthus albus*
(rudely known as pigweed) on the run.
No roots. When a tumbleweed takes off, barbed wire
won't stop it, much less a holstered guard
or signs reading No Unauthorized Vehicles
Beyond This Point. A shuttlebus arrives
after a while to cart you to the reception area,

where people paid to do it teach you how to wait,
with no message, while one shift goes off
and the next comes on, and every half hour or so
you feed another batch of change into a pay phone,
jiggling all the levers of influence you can think of
to no effect whatever.
                                    At a little after
three a.m., finally, Jolene came out—
the same beautiful outrageous gingersnap
with a whole new catalog of indictments.
On the shuttlebus, while a pimp was softly
lecturing his sullen girl on what to do next time,
Jolene described how at the precinct
they'd begun by giving her a
Psychiatric Assessment for which the City
then proceeded to bill her.
By the time the van arrived to take her
to the House of D., the officer
who'd brought her in in the first place
was saying, "Jolene, I love you." And she'd
told him, she told us, exactly what he could do.
All around us in the dark of Riker's Island
the tumbleweeds scurrying were no pigweed,
I was thinking, but the amaranth of antiquity.
And Jolene was not only amaranth and moly, she was poetry
leaping the turnstiles of another century.

SALVAGE

Daily the cortege of crumpled
defunct cars
goes by by the lasagna-
layered flatbed
truckload: hardtop

reverting to tar smudge,
wax shine antiqued to crusted
winepress smear,
windshield battered to
intact ice-tint, a rarity

fresh from the Pleistocene.
I like it; privately
I find esthetic
satisfaction in these
ceremonial removals

from the category of
received ideas
to regions where pigeons'
svelte smoke-velvet
limousines, taxiing

in whirligigs, reclaim
a parking lot,
and the bag-laden
hermit woman, disencumbered
of a greater incubus,

the crush of unexamined
attitudes, stoutly
follows her routine,
mining the mountainsides
of our daily refuse

for artifacts: subversive
re-establishing
with each arcane
trash-basket dig
the pleasures of the ruined.

BALMS

Hemmed in by the prim
deodorizing stare
of the rare-book room,
I stumbled over,
lodged under glass, a
revenant *Essay on Color*
by Mary Gartside, a woman
I'd never heard of, open
to a hand-rendered
watercolor illustration
wet-bright as the day
its unadulterated red-
and-yellow was laid on
(publication date 1818).

Garden nasturtium hues,
the text alongside
explained, had been
her guide. Sudden as
on hands and knees
I felt the smell of them
suffuse the catacomb
so much of us lives in—
horned, pungent, velvet-
eared succulence, a perfume
without hokum, the intimate
of trudging earthworms
and everyone's last end's
unnumbered, milling tenants.

Most olfactory experience
either rubs your nose
in it or tries to flatter
with a funeral home's
approximation of such balms
as a theology of wax alone
can promise, and the bees
deliver. Mary Gartside
died, I couldn't even
learn the year. Our one
encounter occurred by chance
where pure hue set loose
unearthly gusts of odor
from earthbound nasturtiums.

LINDENBLOOM

Before midsummer density
opaques with shade the checker-
tables underneath, in daylight
unleafing lindens burn
green-gold a day or two,
no more, with intimations
of an essence I saw once,
in what had been the pleasure-
garden of the popes
at Avignon, dishevel

into half (or possibly three-
quarters of) a million
hanging, intricately
tactile, blond bell-pulls
of bloom, the in-mid-air
resort of honeybees'
hirsute cotillion
teasing by the milligram
out of those necklaced
nectaries, aromas

so intensely subtle,
strollers passing under
looked up confused,
as though they'd just
heard voices, or
inhaled the ghost
of derelict splendor
and/or of seraphs shaken
into pollen dust
no transubstantiating
pope or antipope could sift
or quite precisely ponder.

THE CORMORANT
IN ITS ELEMENT

That bony potbellied arrow, wing-pumping along
implacably, with a ramrod's rigid adherence,
airborne, to the horizontal, discloses talents
one would never have guessed at. Plummeting

waterward, big black feet splayed for a landing
gear, slim head turning and turning, vermilion-
strapped, this way and that, with a lightning glance
over the shoulder, the cormorant astounding-

ly, in one sleek involuted arabesque, a vertical
turn on a dime, goes into that inimitable
vanishing-and-emerging-from-under-the-briny-

deep act which, unlike the works of Homo Houdini,
is performed for reasons having nothing at all
to do with ego, guilt, ambition, or even money.

CAMOUFLAGE

for Jo and Roy Shaw

It seemed at first like a piece of luck,
the discovery, there in the driveway,
of an odd sort of four-leaf clover—
no bankful of three-penny greenery
but a worried, hovering, wing-dragging
      killdeer's treasury—

a mosaic of four lopsided olives
or marbles you had to hunt
to find again every time, set into
the gravel as if by accident.
We'd have turned that bird's
      entire environment

upside down to have preserved them.
But what was there, after all,
we could have told her about foxes,
coons, cats, or the vandal
with its eye out for whatever anyone
      considers special?

In her bones, in her genes, in
the secret code of her behavior,
she already knew more than all our
bumbling daydreams, our palaver
about safeguards, could muster
      the wit to decipher:

how her whereabouts could vanish
into the gravel, how that brilliant
double-looped necklace could amputate
into invisibility the chevroned
cinnamon of her plumage. Cleverer
        than any mere learned,

merely devious equivocation,
that broken-wing pageant—
who taught her that? We have
no answer except accident,
the trillion-times-over-again
        repeated predicament

sifted with so spendthrift
a disregard for casualties
we can hardly bear to think of
a system so heartless, so shiftless
as being in charge here. It's
        too much like us—

except, after having looked so close
and so long at that casual handful
of dice, squiggle-spotted by luck
that made them half invisible,
watching too often the waltzing swoop
        of the bird's arrival

had meant a disruption of more usual
habits. For all our reading in the papers
about blunderers and risk-takers with
the shrug of nothing-much-matters-
how-those-things-turn-out, we'd unlearned
         to be good losers.

Sorrow, so far as we know, is not
part of a shorebird's equipment.
Nor is memory, of either survival
or losing, after the event.
Having squandered our attention, we
         were less prudent.

For a day, we couldn't quite afford
that morning's black discovery.
Grief is like money: there is only
so much of it we can give away.
And that much grief, for a day,
         bankrupted our economy.

THE KINGFISHER

In a year the nightingales were said to be so loud
they drowned out slumber, and peafowl strolled screaming
beside the ruined nunnery, through the long evening
of a dazzled pub crawl, the halcyon color, portholed
by those eye-spots' stunning tapestry, unsettled
the pastoral nightfall with amazements opening.

Months later, intermission in a pub on Fifty-fifth Street
found one of them still breathless, the other quizzical,
acting the philistine, puncturing Stravinsky—"Tell
me, what *was* that racket in the orchestra about?"—
hauling down the Firebird, harum-scarum, like a kite,
a burnished, breathing wreck that didn't hurt at all.

Among the Bronx Zoo's exiled jungle fowl, they heard
through headphones of a separating panic, the bellbird
reiterate its single *chong,* a scream nobody answered.
When he mourned, "The poetry is gone," she quailed,
seeing how his hands shook, sobered into feeling old.
By midnight, yet another fifth would have been killed.

A Sunday morning, the November of their cataclysm
(Dylan Thomas brought in *in extremis* to St. Vincent's,
that same week, a symptomatic datum) found them
wandering a downtown churchyard. Among its headstones,
while from unruined choirs the noise of Christendom
poured over Wall Street, a benison in vestments,

a late thrush paused, in transit from some grizzled
spruce bog to the humid equatorial fireside: berry-
eyed, bark-brown above, with dark hints of trauma
in the stigmata of its underparts—or so, too bruised
just then to have invented anything so fancy,
later, re-embroidering a retrospect, she had supposed.

In gray England, years of muted recrimination (then
dead silence) later, she could not have said how many
spoiled takeoffs, how many entanglements gone sodden,
how many gaudy evenings made frantic by just one
insomniac nightingale, how many liaisons gone down
screaming in a stroll beside the ruined nunnery;

a kingfisher's burnished plunge, the color
of felicity afire, came glancing like an arrow
through landscapes of untended memory: ardor
illuminating with its terrifying currency
now no mere glimpse, no porthole vista
but, down on down, the uninhabitable sorrow.

THE SMALLER ORCHID

Love is a climate
small things find safe
to grow in—not
(though I once supposed so)
the demanding cattleya
du côté de chez Swann,
glamor among the faubourgs,
hothouse overpowerings, blisses
and cruelties at teatime, but this
next-to-unidentifiable wildling,
hardly more than a
sprout, I've found
flourishing in the hollows
of a granite seashore—
a cheerful tousle, little,
white, down-to-earth orchid
declaring its authenticity,
if you hug the ground
close enough, in a powerful
outdoorsy-domestic
whiff of vanilla.

A HAIRLINE FRACTURE

Whatever went wrong, that week, was more than weather:
a shoddy streak in the fabric of the air of London
that disintegrated into pollen
and came charging down by the bushelful,
an abrasive the color of gold dust, eroding
the tearducts and littering the sidewalks
in the neighborhood of Sloane Square,

where the Underground's upper reaches have the character,
almost, of a Roman ruin—from one
crannied arcade a dustmop of yellow blossom
hung with the stubborn insolence of the unintended,
shaking still other mischief from its hair
onto the platform, the pneumatic haste of missed
trains, the closing barrier—

wherever we went, between fits of sneezing we quarreled:
under the pallid entablatures of Belgravia,
the busy brown façades that were all angles
going in and out like a bellows, even the small house
on Ebury Street where Mozart, at the age of eight,
wrote his first symphony, our difference
was not to be composed.

Unmollified by the freckled plush of mushrooming
monkeyflowers in the windowboxes of Chelsea, undone
by the miraculous rift in the look of things
when you've just arrived—the remote up close,
the knowing that in another, unentered existence
everything shimmering at the surface is this minute
merely, unremarkably familiar—

it was as though we watched the hairline fracture
of the quotidian widen to a geomorphic fissure,
its canyon edge bridged by the rainbows of a terror
that nothing would ever again be right
between us, that wherever we went, nowhere
in the universe would the bone again be knit
or the rift be closed.

EXMOOR

Lost aboard the roll of Kodac-
olor that was to have super-
seded all need to remember
Somerset were: a large flock

of winter-bedcover-thick-
pelted sheep up on the moor;
a stile, a church spire,
and an excess, at Porlock,

of tenderly barbarous antique
thatch in tandem with flowerbeds, relentlessly picturesque, along every sidewalk;

a millwheel; and a millbrook
running down brown as beer.
Exempt from the disaster,
however, as either too quick

or too subtle to put on record, were these: the flutter
of, beside that brown water,
with a butterfly-like flick

of fan-wings, a bright black-
and-yellow wagtail; at Dulver-
ton on the moor, the flavor
of the hot toasted teacake

drowning in melted butter
we had along with a bus-tour-
load of old people; the driver

's way of smothering every *r*
in the wool of a West Countr-
y diphthong, and as a Somer-

set man, the warmth he had for
the high, wild, heather-
dank wold he drove us over.

DANCERS EXERCISING

Frame within frame, the evolving conversation
is dancelike, as though two could play
at improvising snowflakes'
six-feather-vaned evanescence,
no two ever alike. All process
and no arrival: the happier we are,
the less there is for memory to take hold of,
or—memory being so largely a predilection
for the exceptional—come to a halt
in front of. But finding, one evening
on a street not quite familiar,
inside a gated
November-sodden garden, a building
of uncertain provenance,
peering into whose vestibule we were
arrested—a frame within a frame,
a lozenge of impeccable clarity—
by the reflection, no, not
of our two selves, but of
dancers exercising in a mirror,
at the center
of that clarity, what we saw
was not stillness
but movement: the perfection
of memory consisting, it would seem,
in the never-to-be-completed.
We saw them mirroring themselves,
never guessing the vestibule
that defined them, frame within frame,
contained two other mirrors.

SLOW MOTION

Her liquid look as dark
as antique honey,
the auburn of her hide
improbably domestic,
the color of a collie or a
Jersey calf, she occupied
(unantlered, a knob-jointed
monument to mild inquiry)

the total sun of that July
mid-morning. Astonishment
sometimes (as it moved
then) moves slowly
to fill up the heart's abruptly
enormous hollow
with stilled cold
as from a well.

Daring her, I stole
a step. One ear
shifted its ponderous
velour to winnow
what my own bare
tympanum merely spilled
and scattered like
a gust of lost pollen.

The meshes of a life
at close attention
went dense; the heaved
limbs upended slowly,
the white scut half-
lifted in a lopsided
wigwag, as though
even the wildest of
surmises need be
in no great hurry.

SUNDAY MUSIC

The Baroque sewing machine of Georg Friedrich
going back, going back to stitch back together
scraps of a scheme that's outmoded, all
those lopsidedly overblown expectations
now severely in need of revision, re
the nature of things, or more precisely
(back a stitch, back a stitch) the
nature of going forward.

No longer footpath-perpendicular, a monody
tootled on antelope bone, no longer
wheelbarrow heave-ho, the nature of going
forward is not perspective, not stairways,
not, as for the muse of Josquin or Gesualdo,
sostenuto, a leaning together
in memory of, things held onto
fusing and converging,

nor is it any longer an orbit, tonality's
fox-and-goose footprints going round
and round in the snow, the centripetal
force of the dominant. The nature of next
is not what we seem to be hearing
or imagine we feel; is not dance,
is not melody, not elegy,
is not even chemistry,

not Mozart leaching out seraphs
from a sieve of misfortune. The nature
of next is not fugue or rondo, not footpath
or wheelbarrow track, not steamships'
bass vibrations, but less and less
knowing what to expect, it's
the rate of historical
change going faster

and faster: it's noise, it's droids' stone-
deaf intergalactic twitter, it's get ready
to disconnect!—no matter how filled
our heads are with backed-up old
tunes, with polyphony, with basso
profundo fioritura, with this Concerto
Grosso's delectable (back a stitch,
back a stitch) Allegro.

BEETHOVEN, OPUS 111

for Norman Carey

There are epochs . . . when mankind, not con-
tent with the present, longing for time's deeper
layers, like the plowman, thirsts for the virgin
soil of time.

—OSIP MANDELSTAM

—Or, conversely, hungers
for the levitations of the concert hall:
the hands like rafts of *putti*
out of a region where the dolorous stars
are fixed in glassy cerements of Art;
the *ancien régime*'s diaphanous plash
athwart the mounting throb of hobnails—
shod squadrons of vibration
mining the air, its struck ores hardening
into a plowshare, a downward wandering
disrupting every formal symmetry:
from the supine harp-case, the strung-foot
tendons under the mahogany, the bulldozer
in the bass unearths a Piranesian
catacomb: Beethoven ventilating,
with a sound he cannot hear, the cave-in
of recurring rage.

               In the tornado country
of mid-America, my father
might have been his twin—a farmer
hacking at sourdock, at the strangle-
roots of thistles and wild morning glories,
setting out rashly, one October,

to rid the fencerows of poison ivy:
livid seed-globs turreted
in trinities of glitter, ripe
with the malefic glee no farmer doubts
lives deep down things. My father
was naïve enough—by nature
revolutionary, though he'd have
disowned the label—to suppose he might
in some way, minor but radical, disrupt
the givens of existence: set
his neighbors' thinking straight, undo
the stranglehold of reasons nations
send their boys off to war. That fall,
after the oily fireworks had cooled down
to trellises of hairy wicks,
he dug them up, rootstocks and all,
and burned them. Do-gooder!
The well-meant holocaust became
a mist of venom, sowing itself along
the sculptured hollows of his overalls,
braceleting wrists and collarbone—
a mesh of blisters spreading to a shirt
worn like a curse. For weeks
he writhed inside it. Awful.
                              High art
with a stiff neck: an upright Steinway
bought in Chicago; a chromo of a Hobbema
tree-avenue, or of Millet's imagined peasant,
the lark she listens to invisible, perhaps

irrelevant: harpstrings and fripperies of air
congealed into an object nailed against the wall,
its sole ironic function (if it has any)
to demonstrate that one, though he may
grunt and sweat at work, is not a clod.
Beethoven might declare the air
his domicile, the winds kin, the tornado
a kind of second cousin; here,
his labor merely shimmers—a deracinated
album leaf, a bagatelle, the "Moonlight"
rendered with a dying fall (the chords
subside, disintegrate, regroup
in climbing sequences *con brio*); there's
no dwelling on the sweet past here,
there being no past to speak of
other than the setbacks: typhoid
in the wells, half the first settlers
dead of it before a year was out;
diphtheria and scarlet fever
every winter; drought, the Depression,
a mortgage on the mortgage. High art
as a susurrus, the silk and perfume
of unsullied hands. Those hands!—
driving the impressionable wild with anguish
for another life entirely: the Lyceum circuit,
the doomed diving bell of Art.
                                        Beethoven
in his workroom: ear trumpet,
conversation book and pencil, candlestick,

broken crockery, the Graf piano
wrecked by repeated efforts to hear himself—
out of a humdrum squalor the levitations,
the shakes and triplets, the *Adagio*
molto semplice e cantabile, the Arietta
a disintegrating surf of blossom
opening along the keyboard, along the fencerows
the astonishment of sweetness. My father,
driving somewhere in Kansas or Colorado,
in dustbowl country, stopped the car
to dig up by the roots a flower
he'd never seen before—a kind
of prickly poppy most likely, its luminousness
wounding the blank plains like desire.
He mentioned in a letter the disappointment
of his having hoped it might transplant—
an episode that brings me near tears,
still, as even his dying does not—
that awful dying, months-long, hunkered,
irascible. From a clod no plowshare
could deliver, a groan for someone
(because he didn't want to look
at anything) to take away the flowers,
a bawling as of slaughterhouses, slogans
of a general uprising: *Freiheit!*
Beethoven, shut up with the four walls
of his deafness, rehearsing the unhearable
semplice e cantabile, somehow reconstituting
the blister shirt of the intolerable

into these shakes and triplets, a hurrying
into flowering along the fencerows: dying,
for my father, came to be like that
finally—in its messages the levitation
of serenity, as though the spirit might
aspire, in its last act,

                    to walk on air.

PART III

HEARTLAND

The fulcrum of America is the Plains, half sea half land.

—CHARLES OLSON

There is no Middle West. It is a certain climate, a certain land-scape; and beyond that, a state of mind of people born where they do not like to live. —GLENWAY WESCOTT

THE QUARRY

Fishes swam here through the Eocene
too many fathoms up
to think of without suffocation. Light-years
of ooze foreshortened into limestone
swarm with starfish
remoter than the antiquated
pinpoints of astronomy
beneath the stagecoach laboring,
when the thaws came, through mud
up to the hubs. Midsummer's welling bluestem
rose so high the wagons, prairie schooners
under unmasted coifs of canvas,
dragged belly-deep in grass
across the sloughs.
               No roads,
no landmarks to tell where you are,
or who, or whether you will ever find a place
to feel at home in: no alpine
fastness, no tree-profiled pook's hill,
the habitat of magic: only waves
of chlorophyll in motion, the darkened jetsam
of bur oaks, a serpentine of willows
along the hollows—a flux
that waterlogs the mind, draining southeastward
by osmosis to the Mississippi,
where by night the body of De Soto,
ballasted with sand—or was it armor?—
sank into the ooze, nudged by the barbels,
as it decomposed, of giant catfish. Others,

in a terrain as barren
as the dust of bones, kept the corrupt
obsession going: Gold—greed for the metal
most prized because by nature it's
least corruptible. Flushed finally
out of the heartland drainpipe,
the soft parts of De Soto's body filtered
into the capillaries of the delta.   Will
some shard of skull or jawbone, undecomposed,
outlast his name, as the unquarried starfish
outlast the seas that inundated them?
                                        Think back
a little, to what would have been
without this festering of lights at night,
this grid of homesteads, this hardening
lymph of haste foreshortened into highways:
the lilt and ripple of the dark,
birdsong at dusk augmented by frog choirs
already old before the Eocene; the wickiups
now here, now there, edged westward
year by year, hemmed in or undermined,
done in finally by treaties. The year
the first land office in the territory opened,
when there were still no roads
other than wagon tracks, one Lyman Dillon,
starting at Dubuque, drove a plow southwestward
a hundred miles—the longest furrow
ever, straight into the belly of the future,
where the broken loam would soon

be mounted, as on a howdah, by
a marble capitol, the glister
of whose dome still overtops
the frittered sprawl of who we are,
of where we came from,
with its stilted El Dorado.

THE WOODLOT

Clumped murmuring above a sump of loam—
grass-rich, wood-poor—that first the plow,
then the inventor (his name plowed under
somewhere in the Patent Office) of barbed wire,
taught, if not fine manners, how at least to follow
the surveyor's rule, the woodlot nodes of willow,
evergreen or silver maple gave the prairie grid
what little personality it had.
                              Who could
have learned fine manners where the air,
that rude nomad, still domineered,
without a shape it chose to keep,
oblivious of section lines, in winter
whisking its wolfish spittle to a froth
that turned whole townships into
one white wallow? Barbed wire
kept in the cattle but would not abrade
the hide or draw the blood
of gales hurled gnashing like seawater over fences'
laddered apertures, rigging the landscape
with the perspective of a shipwreck. Land-chained,
the blizzard paused to caterwaul
at every windbreak, a rage the worse
because it was in no way personal.
                              Against
the involuted tantrums of spring and summer—
sackfuls of ire, the frightful udder
of the dropped mammocumulus
become all mouth, a lamprey

swigging up whole farmsteads, suction
dislodging treetrunks like a rotten tooth—
luck and a cellarhole were all
a prairie dweller had to count on.
                                        Whether
the inventor of barbed wire was lucky
finally in what he found himself
remembering, who knows? Did he
ever, even once, envision
the spread of what he'd done
across a continent: whale-song's
taut dulcimer still thrumming as it strung together
orchard, barnyard, bullpen, feedlot,
windbreak: wire to be clambered over,
crawled through or slid under, shepherded—
the heifers staring—to an enclosure
whose ceiling's silver-maple tops
stir overhead, uneasy, in the interminably
murmuring air? Deep in it, under
appletrees like figures in a ritual, violets
are thick, a blue cellarhole
of pure astonishment.
                                It is
the earliest memory. Before it,
I/you, whatever that conundrum may yet
prove to be, amounts to nothing.

IMAGO

Sometimes, she remembers, a chipped flint
would turn up in a furrow,
pink as a peony (from the iron in it)
or as the flared throat of a seashell:
a nomad's artifact fished from the broth,
half sea half land—hard evidence
of an unfathomed state of mind.

Nomads. The wagon train that camped
and left its name on Mormon Ridge.
The settlers who moved on to California,
bequeathing a laprobe pieced from the hide
of a dead buffalo, the frail sleigh
that sleeps under the haymow, and a headstone
so small it might be playing house,
for the infant daughter, aged two days,
no name, they also left behind.

Half sea half land: the shirker propped
above her book in a farmhouse parlor
lolls with the merfolk who revert to foam,
eyeing at a distance the lit pavilions
that seduced her, their tailed child,
into the palaces of metamorphosis. She pays
now (though they do not know this)
by treading, at every step she takes,
on a parterre of tomahawks.

A thirst for something definite so dense
it feels like drowning. Grant Wood
turned everything to cauliflower,

the rounded contours of a thunderhead,
flint-hard. He made us proud:
though all those edges might not be quite
the way it was, at least he'd tried.

"But it has no form!" they'd say to
the scribbler whose floundering fragments
kept getting out of hand—and who, either
fed up with or starved out of
her native sloughs, would, stowed aboard
the usual nomadic moving van, trundle her
dismantled sensibility elsewhere.

Europe, that hodgepodge of ancestral
calamities, was hard and handsome, its rubble
confident, not shriveling on the vine,
as here, like an infertile melon—the Virgin
jejune in her grotto of cold plaster, half sick
of that sidelong enclave, the whispered "Cathlick."

Antiquity unshrouds on wimpling canvas,
adjunct of schoolhouse make-believe: the Italy
of urns and cypresses, of stairways
evolving toward a state of mind
not to be found except backstage
among hunchbacks and the miscreants
who control the scenery, flanked
by a pair of masks whose look, at even
this remove, could drill through bone:
the tragic howl, the comic rictus,
eyeholes that stare out of the crypt

of what no grownup is ever heard to speak of
but in the strangled tone whose lexicon
is summed up in one word: *Bankrupt.*

Bankrupt: the abysm of history,
a slough to be pulled out of
any way you could. Antiquity, the backward
suction of the dark, amounted to a knothole
you plugged with straw, old rags, pages
ripped from last year's Sears Roebuck catalog,
anything, to ward off the blizzard.

Not so, for the born-again, the
shuddering orifices of summer.
On prayer-meeting night, outside
the vestibule among multiple
bell-pulls of Virginia creeper,
the terrible clepsydra of becoming
distils its drop: a luna moth, the emblem
of the born-again, furred like an orchid
behind the ferned antennae, a totem-
garden of lascivious pheromones,
hangs, its glimmering streamers
pierced by the dripstone burin of the eons
with the predatory stare out of the burrow,
those same eyeholes. Imago
of unfathomable evolvings, living
only to copulate and drop its litter,
does it know what it is, what it has been,
what it may or must become?

THE LOCAL GENIUS

SPACE (spelled large) the central fact:
thus Charles Olson. For Glenway Wescott,
the state of mind of those who never liked
to live where they were born—all that
utilitarian muck down underfoot,
brown loam, debris of grassroots packed
thicker than anywhere else on the planet—
soil, so much of it that the central fact

must be, after all, not SPACE but DIRT,
forever present as the sense of guilt
washday alone can hope to expiate.
With what Will Voss of Davenport
invented, the Maytags of Newton built
a dynasty on getting rid of it.

STACKING THE STRAW

In those days the oatfields'
fenced-in vats of running platinum,
the yellower alloy of wheat and barley,
whose end, however gorgeous all that trammeled
rippling in the wind, came down
to toaster-fodder, cereal
as a commodity, were a rebuke
to permanence—to bronze or any metal
less utilitarian than the barbed braids
that marked off a farmer's property,
or the stoked dinosaur of a steam engine
that made its rounds from farm to farm,
after the grain was cut and bundled,
and powered the machine that did the threshing.

Strawstacks' beveled loaves, a shape
that's now extinct, in those days were
the nearest thing the region had
to monumental sculpture. While hayracks
and wagons came and went, delivering bundles,
carting the winnowed ore off to the granary,

a lone man with a pitchfork stood aloft
beside the hot mouth of the blower,
building about himself, forkful
by delicately maneuvered forkful,
a kind of mountain, the golden
stuff of mulch, bedding for animals.
I always thought of him with awe—

a craftsman whose evolving altitude
gave him the aura of a hero. He'd come down
from the summit of the season's effort
black with the baser residues of that
discarded gold. Saint Thomas of Aquino
also came down from the summit
of a lifetime's effort, and declared
that everything he'd ever done was straw.

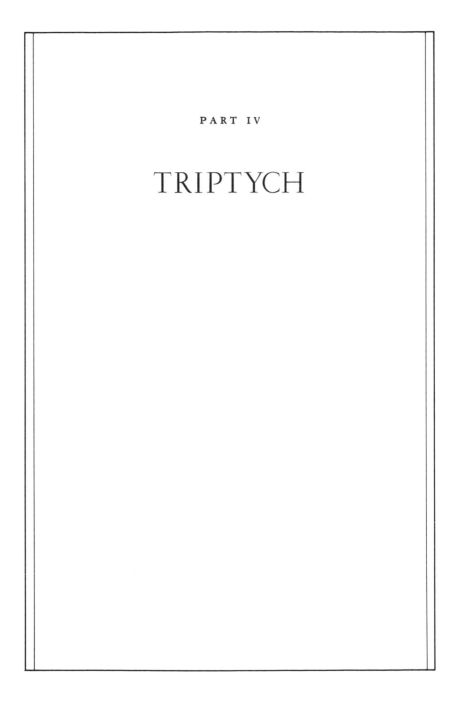

PART IV

TRIPTYCH

PALM SUNDAY

Neither the wild tulip, poignant
and sanguinary, nor the dandelion
blowsily unbuttoning, answers
the gardener's imperative, if need be,
to maim and hamper in the name of order,
or the taste for rendering adorable
the torturer's implements—never mind
what entrails, not yet trampled under
by the feet of choirboys (sing,
my tongue, the glorious battle),
mulch the olive groves, the flowering
of apple and almond, the boxwood
corridor, the churchyard yew,
the gallows tree.

GOOD FRIDAY

Think of the Serengeti lions looking up,
their bloody faces no more culpable
than the acacia's claw on the horizon
of those yellow plains: think with what
concerted expertise the red-necked,
down-ruffed vultures take their turn,
how after them the feasting maggots
hone the flayed wildebeest's ribcage
clean as a crucifix—a thrift tricked out
in ribboned rags, that looks like waste—
and wonder what barbed whimper, what embryo
of compunction, first unsealed the long
compact with a limb-from-limb outrage.

Think how the hunting cheetah, from
the lope that whips the petaled garden
of her hide into a sandstorm, falters,
doubling back, nagged by a lookout
for the fuzzed runt that can't
keep up, that isn't going to make it,
edged by a niggling in the chromosomes
toward these garrulous, uneasy caravans
where, eons notwithstanding, silence
still hands down the final statement.

Think of Charles Darwin mulling over
whether to take out his patent on
the way the shape of things can alter,
hearing the whir, in his own household,

of the winnowing fan no system
(it appears) can put a stop to,
winnowing out another little girl,
for no good reason other than
the docile accident of the unfit,
before she quite turned seven.

Think of his reluctance to disparage
the Wedgwood pieties he'd married into,
his more-than-inkling of the usages
disinterested perception would be put to:
think how, among the hard-nosed, pity
is with stunning eloquence converted
to hard cash: think how Good Friday
can, as a therapeutic outlet, serve
to ventilate the sometimes stuffy
Lebensraum of laissez-faire society:

an ampoule of gore, a mithridatic
ounce of horror—sops for the maudlin
tendency of women toward extremes
of stance, from virgin blank to harlot
to sanctimonious official mourner—
myrrh and smelling salts, baroque
placebos, erotic tableaux vivants
dedicated to the household martyr,
underwriting with her own ex votos
the evolving ordonnance of murder.

The spearpoint glitters in the gorge:
wonder, at Olduvai, what innovator,
after the hunting cat halfway sniffed out
remorse in the design of things,
unsatisfied perhaps with even a lion's
entitlement, first forged the iron
of a righteousness officially exempt
from self-dismay: think, whatever
rueful thumbprint first laid the rubric
on the sacerdotal doorpost, whose victim,
knowing, died without a murmur,
how some fragment of what shudders,
lapped into that crumpled karma,
dreams that it was once a tiger.

EASTER MORNING

a stone at dawn
cold water in the basin
these walls' rough plaster
imageless
after the hammering
of so much insistence
on the need for naming
after the travesties
that passed as faces,
grace : the unction
of sheer nonexistence
upwelling in this
hyacinthine freshet
of the unnamed
the faceless

PART V

WATERSHEDS

MARGINAL EMPLOYMENT

The Duc de Berry usually wore a robe
the color of the Mediterranean, and listed
two pots of salts of cobalt
along with apes and dromedaries,
a tooth of Charlemagne, another
from a narwhal, and a charred snippet
from the mantle of the prophet,
among his choicest curios.

Though unacquainted with the works
of Marx, he added value
to the hours of no one knows
how many lapidaries, couturiers,
embroiderers of passementerie
with gilt and pearls, and wielders
in gold leaf of the minutest
marginal punctilio. The progress
of his *Très Riches Heures*
is burdened with a fossil gilding
not only of the lily but also of the even
finer flower of the grass, which goes

clothed nowadays in common purple—
nerve-nets of tressed fertility,
marginal fan-vaultings scintillating
with a sequin rain: out of what matrix
of pounded relics, what impastos'
thickened blood and mire, the scandal
of such squandered ornament, no less

than any artifice uniquely crafted
for an emperor's enjoyment, escapes
our mere totting-up. The earth's hours
are weightier, for all this lightness,
than the sum of human enterprise's
tumbledown fiascos, and the burden
of the oceans' robe, unlike the air
it takes the color of, is more ponderous
than greed, although
it flows, it flows, it flows.

TEPOZTLÁN

The Aztecs, conquering, brought Huitzilopochtli
and ceremonial slitting the heart out; Cortés,
a.k.a. Son of the Sun, along with new weapons,
El Señor and the Virgin of the Remedies,
introduced heaven and hell (which the Tepoztecans
never quite took hold of); the gringos
arrived with sanitary arrangements
and a great many questions.
                        Autonomy
climbed down from the plane empty-handed,
carrying only introspection and a few
self-canceling tropisms, innocent
of history as any peasant, to travel,
all in a day, from upland maguey fields'
clumped pewter prongs through treetop regions
where songbirds bright as parrots flashed
uncaged, living free as fishes; alongside
churches of ice-cream-tinted stone
carved like a barbed music, and vendors
of a poisoned rainbow—*helados, refrescos,*
nopals, papayas, mangos, melons all swarming
with warned-against amoebas—down
through villages smelling of pulque,
jasmine and dysentery; past haciendas
torpid with dust, the dogs owned by nobody,
the burros, whether led or tethered, all
long-suffering rancor, the stacked coffins
waiting, mainly child-size (fatality,
part jaguar, part hummingbird, part

gila monster, alive and well here,
clearly needs children); through the daily
dust-laying late-afternoon rainstorm,
in cadenced indigenous place-names
the drip of a slow waterfall,
or of foliage when the rain stops—
arriving, just after sundown,
at the town of Tepoztlán.

                         Autonomy,
unaware that in some quarters
the place was famous, saw hanging
cliffs dyed a terrible heart-color
in the gloaming light; a marketplace
empty of people; a big double-towered
church whose doors stood open. No one
inside but a sexton in white *calzoni*,
sweeping up a litter that appeared
to be mainly jasmine: so much fragrance,
so much death, such miracles—El Señor,
glitter-skirted, casketed upright in glass—
such silence . . . until, for no known reason,
overhead the towered bells broke out
into such a pounding that bats, shaken
from their hooked-accordion sleep
by the tumult, poured onto the dark,
a river of scorched harbingers
from an underworld the Tepoztecans
don't altogether believe in.

                         They speak

on occasion of Los Aires, or, in their
musical Nahuatl, of *Huehuetzintzin,*
the Old Ones. Who knows what ultimately
is, and what's mere invention? Autonomy,
encapsuled and enmembraned hitherto
by a deaf anxiety, left Tepoztlán
marked, for the first time ever,
by the totally unlooked-for—by a
halfway belief that from out there,
astoundingly, there might be,
now and then, some message.

REMEMBERING GREECE

for Peter Kybart

At noon in this blue cove of the Atlantic
a stiff breeze gets up, exactly as you've seen
it do off Delos. Poseidon, to whose unease
mumbling Delphi purported to assign some meaning,

is quiescent here. Snoring under northern shores,
the Earth-Disturber has hardly more than whimpered
since, enrobed in thickening catastrophes of ice,
the drowned once-mountaintops of this red granite

all but suffocated in his bath—today so blue,
it halfway dislocates itself to the Aegean
and becomes, if only in the way events can weigh
upon events, the bloodied bath of Agamemnon.

THE RESERVOIRS
OF MOUNT HELICON

The monks are dying out at Hosios Loukas.
At Great Vespers the celebrant,
singing alone in a cracked ancient voice
while I hug the stall, sole auditor,
keeps losing his place in the chant-book's
stiff curled parchment. Having come by taxi
all the way from Delphi (the driver waits
outside, in no hurry) to be mowed down by a tsunami
of Greek voices, I experience only
the onset of an urge to giggle.
                              The mosaics
are hardly up to the postcards; tourists,
now that there's a highway, arrive
by the busload. But the ride up—
wet appletrees' cusp-studded wands
aped by the unlikely topside hue of crows
braking and turning just below eye level—
is worth it, and so are the plane trees
that grow here: huge as churches,
they might go back a thousand years, be older
than Hosios Loukas, whose hermitage this was,
be older even than Luke the painter
of seraphic epiphanies. He'd have found it
strange here: the light all muzzy silver,
Helicon green and vast across a mist-
hung gorge, these plane trees
so palpably, venerably pagan—
but I think he might have liked it.
                              Waiting

outside for the vesper bell, I fell into
conversation with a monk—one of fifteen
now remaining, he told me—who spoke a kind
of English learned, and since largely forgotten,
during a sojourn in Brooklyn. They'd been building
a bridge then, he recalled, across the Hudson;
he supposed it must be finished by now.
I told him, in a faint voice, yes,
it had been finished—and looked out, whelmed
into vertigo by gulfs spanned for a moment
by so mere a thread, across a gorge
already half-imaginary with distance
toward the improbable, the muse-haunted
reservoirs of Mount Helicon.

TRASIMENE

Tourmaline plashing in a noose of reeds,
Lake Trasimene is being slowly strangled
in ecology, no respecter of the Quattrocento.
How could that sheeted
opacity be looked at, after Arezzo,
except as the filtered tint,
wet lake-hue into fresco, Piero
della Francesca laid like rain
over sky, drapery, the roofs of houses?
How, after Perugia, after the Louvre
and the Uffizi, can the Umbria
of Perugino be seen, five centuries later,
except as he pre-empted it?—as space
looking inward, transparency set breathing
to commend an attitude: Madonna,
head drooping like a tulip, among donors.
Fashions in felicity play hide and seek
with decor; reigning apostolates
shrink to a simper. It's the lake's
look that breathes here,
infinity's eutrophic emerald
that won't keep either.

RAIN AT BELLAGIO

for Doris Thompson Myers

I

The omnipresence of the sound of water: rain
on the graveled walks, the lakeside terraces,
the red pantiles of Bellagio.

At Paestum we had not heard it.
An acreage of thyme, winnowed by sea breezes.
A line of blue out past the silted harbor—
unauthenticated because unheard,
a scene one might have dreamed.

At Herculaneum, a stoppage of the ears.
Cicadas mute, an oleander stillness.
Rancor of cypresses. Impacted fire.
Effete ribaldry strangling in hot mud
up to the nostrils. Water stricken
from the ledgers of memory.

At Naples, human noise inundating the bayfront,
lapping at castles' elephantine hooves, rampaging
tenement ravines. Once in the night
I woke and knew it had been raining—
not from the sound but from the smell, as though
an animal had left its spoor.

Under an aspect less clement, the trickle
of sewers, the vine-patched bombholes,

bambini with no underpants, gnarled women
wearing the black of perpetual resignation,
might have figured more gravely than as a condiment,
garlic for a week of living well.

2

Aboard the *wagons-lits* we drank Est! Est! Est!,
leaned tipsily out of windows, behaved
as though we owned the railway car, owned
the platform as it receded, owned even, overhead,
the diminution to a half-perceived scintilla
of the stars, after the manner of the young who travel
Europe, garnering experience in pairs.

We passed the Apennines asleep, and woke in a country
where the color of the olive trees was rainy.
Gray rain muddying the emerald of ricefields,
blurring, across the flood plain of the Po, the vague
geometry of poplars on the march—a part
of some interminable uprising.

At Milan a drizzle, the boulevards inlaid
with dun-colored patines, the slough of plane trees.
A car sent from the villa, behind whose steamed windows
we talk as freely as though the driver had no ears.
Glimpsing, through sheets of rain, the first gray-green,

narrow windings of Lake Como,
the red pantiles of Monza and Lecco,
the little farms, the villa walls
sequestering unimagined pleasures. Vineyards.
Terraces. The starred darkness of lemon trees
through the downpour. Gravel under our shoes,
a footman holding an umbrella. All as in
that terrifying place where no one is admitted
whose taste is not impeccable.

3

Servants. The butler's practiced deference,
the liquid glance unerring as a falcon's—
a lisp in the shrubbery, a blur of wingbars
and he's placed you. On the hall table
tuberoses' opening racemes purport a sadness
the equal of Elysium. Massed carnations
in a cushioned bedroom, a bath overlooking
the flutter of chaffinches, cypresses'
columned melancholy, the lacquered foliage
of magnolias seen from the balcony, are no refuge
from the surveillance of chambermaids, scathing
as a penitent's examination of conscience.
The scuffed suitcase cannot escape: as soon as
your back is turned, they have
already unpacked it.

Out on the lake a white traghetto, moving
almost without pause from one shore to the other,
a punctual amphibious spider, skeins
into one zigzag the descending
clatter from the campaniles of Bellagio,
of Varenna and Cadenabbia, as though reining
the fragments of experience into one process—
being-and-becoming fused, a single scheme.

The rustle of descending silk (these shores
being mulberry country), the curtains drawn
against the prerogative of the chambermaids,
behind closed doors, having had our tea,
conspiratorially, two high-church Episcopalians, we begin
to read aloud the office of Compline.

The damask weave of luxury, the arras
of melodrama. A wailing about the eaves.
Confidences wading like a salvage operation
toward an untidy past: the admirer
who had in fact been a bricklayer,
who wore dirty undershirts; the rue
of not-yet-dealt-with gaffes, chagrins
and false positions, tinder
for the scorn of maître d's, the pained
look of a host whose taste is impeccable:
hazards of a murderous civility, the beast
snared in a nightmare of living well.

4

Cocktails in the salotto, underneath a portrait
of the late owner, a distiller's heiress
of dim but cultivated beauty, whose third spouse
left her title to an extinct principality. The villa,
acquired by caprice, became her favorite household.
Though in the way of moral character not much
is to be expected, *noblesse oblige*: the servants—
eighty of them altogether—must be provided for.
Emissaries of those foundations into which
the larger fortunes have unavoidably been siphoned
were circuitously whispered to; and so, the times
being what they have become, the princeliest
of the seventeen bedrooms, stripped
of its cushier urgings to dalliance,
is now a conference room—this week
for a conclave of jurisprudes, the week after
for experts in the field of public health
concerning the eradication of malaria.

Reclamation of the land: the labor gangs,
the overseers, the seasonal migrations,
the Lombard plain at last made habitable,
a source of fortunes: irrigated water meadows,
ricefields, wheat, mulberries, the channeled music
of the Po, the Oglio, the Adda, the Ticino. Vineyards.
Landed estates. Walled properties above Lake Como,
for the view. A rural proletariat whose fortunes
and miseries go unrecorded.

5

In her declining years the Principessa
was to be seen leaning, as she made her rounds
nuzzled in sable against the lake damp,
on the arm of her butler.

The indispensable tyranny of servants.
Gardeners, kitchen maids, woodcutters, grooms,
footmen. Private secretaries.
Confessors. Archbishops.
Above the fever trap of the Maremma
the ritual complicity: in castle towers
the secret stair, the cached aconite,
the hired assassin.

Fiefdoms. Latifundia. The wealth of nations.
The widening distance between rich and poor,
between one branch and another of the tree of misery.
A view of lakeside terraces
to sell one's soul for.

6

Among the company at dinner, Professor B.,
reputedly the best mind in Italy,
who speaks no English; also Professor d'E.,
who speaks it more exquisitely than any native—
slim, fair, elfin, author of a legal treatise

no one (he says) has read.
　　　—Then I will read it.
　　　—Oh, but really it is very dull.
The weather in Italy, he says, is changing.
Now that charcoal is no longer burned
extensively, the forests have grown up again,
forests draw moisture—*Ecco!*

Flooding along the Po, the Adige, the Ticino.
Dykes giving way at Ferrara, inundations
at Rimini, the beetfields of Ravenna
already under water. On the flood plain,
the mosaics of Sant' Apollinare in Classe
ripple as though drowned—redemption
envisioned as a wall of water.

　　　　　　　　7

What does a place like this not offer?
Flawless cuisine, a first-rate cellar,
mountain footpaths laced with wild cyclamen
and maidenhair; topiary, sunken gardens,
wood nymphs and a dying slave in marble; even,
when nothing short of total solitude
will do, a hermitage.

My friend is twenty,
blond as Lucrezia Borgia, her inclinations

nurtured with care since childhood.
She speaks three languages and has had
six proposals. Since January
her existence has been an exercise
in living like a Principessa. Her father
still cannot fathom what has happened.
He points, appealing, to a letter
on the hall table, overhung
by the tuberoses' extravagant love-death,
addressed to an abbess.

And will she be free to leave if she should wish to?
He, for one, does not believe it. They will wear her down
in that enclosed community, those Anglican Benedictines.
She will become nothing other than a model prisoner.
That, as he understands it, is the long and short
of what what they call *formation* amounts to.

One might have said by way of a response (but did not)
that living under vows, affianced to a higher poverty,
might likewise be an exercise in living well.

8

Her last evening amounts to an exercise in prevarication.
Where precisely she is going, and why, she has
given up explaining. Dinner is a banquet. Afterward,
half sozzled on red wine followed by champagne

followed by Strega, we're in raincoats,
climbing into a villa car with a pair
of half-fledged jurisprudes. A halt
somewhere along the way, the rain slackening
and closing in again like trees in a landscape,
to snitch grapes from a vineyard. We arrive
at the farewell party pretending we're bacchantes.

Antique U.S. jazz on a portable phonograph.
Liqueurs. Chocolates. My friend dancing
the cha-cha-cha, engaging in mock flirtations
with a moody Italian, then with a cheerful one
whose profession entails the proliferation of supermarkets.
     —But how *can* you?
     —And why isn't what's good for your country
       good also for Italy?

A prolonged huddle with the cheerful one. Emerging,
they announce they have an announcement:
they have decided to get married
for about a week. At midnight,
trying for a departure, we find the door
locked against us, the key hidden prettily
in somebody's décolletage. Everybody
is going away tomorrow. We say goodbye
to the jurisprudes, the young footman
standing expressionless beside the door.

9

The pang of bells, through rain-filled dark,
at every hour. Half slumber,
feeble morning light. At seven, booted
and raincoated, we're plunging through the wet
to board the traghetto—the only passengers,
along with a truckload of Italian beer—for Cadenabbia
and early communion at the English church.

A port, a buoy, a rudder: hymnbook similes
capsize in the act of kneeling
and receiving the substance of such controversy,
cataclysms from the winepress of the glaciers,
whatever it is that knows itself only
in the sense of being carried,
all the bridges out, surrounded
by the rush of moving water—total
self-abandonment perceived as living well.

A rush for the landing, the water rushing alongside,
down gutters, over cobblestones. In one hour
the level of the lake has risen astoundingly.
Aboard the traghetto, a priest
wears a violet-lined biretta
and buckles on his shoes.

Seeing how the picturesque outlives its meaning.

10

Punctually at three in the afternoon, our luggage
waits by the door, the car stands in the rain,
its motor running. Bathos of tuberoses
on the hall table, the butler's formal bow,
the footman holding an umbrella. Gravel
under our shoes. Behind the steamed windows
confidences interspersed with silences.
At Milan, dim through fatigue, a watershed:
for the rest of our lives, we will be traveling
in opposite directions. Behind us, limestone
and chestnut mountainsides, streaming, release
their increment of moisture: rain, glacier melt,
the wine of change. Ahead of us,
spilling across the lap of Italy, the tributaries
of the Po—the Adda, the Oglio, the Sesia—
mingle and descend toward Ferrara,
toward Rimini and Ravenna: uncontrollable
as rumor, as armies set in motion,
the sound of water.

11

Sometimes since, in dreams I find myself obliged
to assume, without previous instruction, control
of a plane I have no memory of boarding. I wake
without ever having learned the outcome. Or,

in another region, I find myself
face to face with the transparent strata
of experience, the increment of years,
as a wall of inundation, the drowned mosaic
glimmering above the flood plain. Waking,
I hear the night sounds merge, a single rustle
as of silk, as though becoming might amend,
unbroken, to one stilled, enclosing skein.

12

At the Abbey, between the shored-up Norman church
and the trefoiled oak of the pilgrim hostel,
running liquid and garrulous through a life of silence,
cushioned and tended between banks of tamed wildflowers,
the sound of water: indivisible, unstilled,
unportioned by the bells that strike the hours.

PART VI

HYDROCARBON

OR CONSIDER PROMETHEUS

In 1859 petroleum was discovered in Pennsylvania. Kerosene, petroleum, and paraffin began rapidly to replace whale oil, sperm oil,
and spermaceti wax. . . . Consider whaling
as FRONTIER, and INDUSTRY. A product wanted,
men got it: big business. The Pacific as sweat-
shop . . . the whaleship as factory, the whale-
boat the precision instrument. . . .

—CHARLES OLSON, *Call Me Ishmael*

I

Would Prometheus, cursing on his rock
as he considered fire, the smuggled gem
inside the weed stem, and the excesses
since his protracted punishment began,

have cursed the ocean's copious antidote,
its lapping, cold, incessant undulance
plowed to shards by wheeling porpoises,
hydrogen-cum-oxygen fanned up in mimicries

of hard carbon, diamond of purest water,
the unforbidden element crosscut by fire,
its breakup the absolving smile of rainbows?
Or, considering leviathan, whose blameless

progenitors turned from the shore, from its
seducing orchards, renouncing the prehensile
dangle of a brain all eyes and claws,
twittering fishhook strategies of grasp

and mastery, for immersion among moving
declivities, have envied the passivity
whose massive ease is no more than his own
tormented rectitude, immune from drowning?

2

How would the great cetaceans, Houyhnhnm
intelligences sans limbs, ungoaded by
the Promethean monkeyshines that gave us
haute cuisine, autos-da-fé and fireworks,

dining al fresco off cuttlefish and krill,
serving up baleen-strained plankton, whose
unmanipulative ears explore Olympian parterres
of sonar, devise the ringing calculus

of icebergs, compute the density of ships
as pure experience of hearing—how
would these basking reservoirs of fuel,
wax and glycerine have read the trypots

readied for their rendering into tallow
for a thousand candles? How, astronomers
of the invisible, would they have tracked
the roaring nimbus of that thieving

appetite, our hunger for the sun, or
charted the harrowing of jet and piston
pterodactyls, robots fed on their successor,
fire-drinking vampires of hydrocarbon?

THE ANNIVERSARY

SEPTEMBER 1, 1939

Night after night of muffled
rant, of tumefying apprehension
impended like a marriage
all through the summer—larger
even, for one as yet without
consensual knowledge, than
the act of love.

The weather that last weekend
at the Crescent Beach Hotel
went bad. Lake Okoboji, under
a tarpaulin of overcast (bare
springboard, all the rowboats
idle) turned pale, then
darkened to gunmetal.

A lolling weekend foursome,
unwelcomed as wet weather,
tainted the family dinner hour
with a scurrilous good humor
as of having, without compunction,
already seen how far the arson
in our common nature
would choose to go.

The meaning of the evening newscast,
no news, confirmed the reluctant

off-color miracle that had
made the summer pregnant.
Ultimatums had brought forth
their armored litter; Poland
had witnessed even now,
in darkness, the beginning
of the burning.

Rain roared down all night,
unstoppable as war, onto
the stricken porches of
the Crescent Beach Hotel.
Lightning through the downpour
repeatedly divebombed the water
like an imagined lover.

Arson, a generation's habitual
dolor, observes its anniversary,
its burning birthday, its passage
from an incendiary overture
to what the ignorance of that
September, of this September
minus forty, would
consent to know.

LETTERS FROM JERUSALEM

Engines of burning took him there
and brought back the first postcard,
a view of Jerusalem. The high air
swam with domes, their drowned gilding
glimmering like live fish scales.
The sky at night was an aquarium
of light-years whose distances
at noon, converging, turned the desert
        to burning glass.

The kibbutzim aren't quite, he admits,
what he'd expected. The Talmud
couldn't care less about anybody's
happiness. But is that (he writes)
even important? Perhaps the true
arrival is always inward? He walks
the hills, the clogged bazaars,
everywhere. He is learning Hebrew.
        Immerse, immerse—

inward but also downward. He sees
time impend, the weather changing.
Clouds mass on the horizon; daylight
shrinks backward to the Maccabees'
last reckoning. In secret, from
the squalid rigor of the Yeshiva
and his unheated room, he flees
with Saint-Exupéry into regions
        of wind, sand and stars.

Immersion, thirst for roots, the passion
of expecting less: he asks now (he writes)
no more than to be here as a witness.
He begins even to dream in Hebrew:
locutions bend as though half in,
half out of water. But the watershed
that waits is made of fire: a cherub
in the doorway poses the blazing
            conundrum of the Jews

whose Biblical injunction is: if he stays
he must go into the army. The 'sixties
subversive pacifist he was must unadopt
that arrogance or lose Jerusalem.
A bush burned once; volcanoes
tutored the patriarchs; Elijah
was taken up in rafts of flame.
From Moscow, rumors arrive of new
            pogroms. He stays.

The latest letter, with no date, begins
Shalom! Tomorrow his leave ends,
then back to the desert. Tanks are less
accommodating even than the Talmud
to a divided mind. The promised land
more and more is dense with engines.
Converging overhead, in skies that swam,
the distances grow predatory and explode
            with burning seraphim.

BERCEUSE

Listen to Gieseking playing a Berceuse
of Chopin—the mothwing flutter
light as ash, perishable as burnt paper—

and sleep, now the furnaces of Auschwitz
are all out, and tourists go there.
The purest art has slept with turpitude,

we all pay taxes. Sleep. The day of waking
waits, cloned from the phoenix—
a thousand replicas in upright silos,

nurseries of the ultimate enterprise.
Decay will undo what it can, the rotten
fabric of our repose connives with doomsday.

Sleep on, scathed felicity. Sleep, rare
and perishable relic. Imagining's no shutter
against the absolute, incorrigible sunrise.

THE DAHLIA GARDENS

There are places no history can reach.
—NORMAN MAILER, *Armies of the Night*

Outside the river entrance, between the Potomac
and the curbed flowerbeds, a man walks up and down,
has been walking this last half hour. November leaves
skip in the wind or are lifted, unresisting,
to mesh with the spent residue of dahlias'
late-summer blood and flame, leached marigolds,
knives of gladioli flailed to ribbons:
parts of a system that seems, on the face of it,
to be all waste, entropy, dismemberment;
but which perhaps, given time enough, will prove
to have refused nothing tangible,
                              enjambed
without audible clash, with no more than a whiplash
incident, to its counterpart, a system
shod in concrete, cushioned in butyl, riding
chariots of thermodynamics, adept with the unrandom,
the calculus of lifting and carrying, with vectors,
clocks, chronicles, calibrations.
                              File clerks
debouch into the dusk—it is rush hour; headlights
thicken, a viscous chain along the Potomac—
from concentric corridors, five sides
within five sides, grove leading on to grove
lit by autonomous purrings, daylight
on demand, dense with the pristine,

the dead-white foliage of those archives
that define and redefine with such precision,
such subtleties of exactitude, that only
the honed mind's secret eye can verify
or vouch for its existence, how the random
is to be overcome, the unwelcome
forestalled, the arcane calamity
at once refused, delineated and dwelt on. Where,
as here, triune Precaution, Accumulation
and Magnitude obtain, such levitations
and such malignities have come, with time,
to seem entirely natural—this congeries
being unquestionably the largest
office building in Christendom.
                              The man alone
between blackened flowerbeds and the blackening
Potomac moves with care, as though balanced
astride the whiplash between system and system—
wearing an overcoat, hatless, thinning-haired,
a man of seemingly mild demeanor
who might have been a file clerk
were it not for his habit of writing down
notes to himself on odd scraps of paper,
old bills, the backs of envelopes, or in a notebook
he generally forgets to bring with him,
and were it not for the wine jug
he carries (the guard outside the river entrance,
as he pauses, has observed it, momentarily puzzled)
cradled close against his overcoat.

By now file clerks,
secretaries, minor and major bureaucrats, emerging
massively through the several ports of egress,
along the ramps, past the walled flowerbeds,
which the lubrications and abrasions of routine,
the multiple claims of a vigilant anxiety,
the need for fine tuning, for continual
readjustment of expectation, have rendered
largely negligible, flow around him.
He moves against the flux, toward the gardens.
Around him, leaves skip in the wind
like a heartbeat, like a skipped
heartbeat

       if I were a dead leaf
       thou mightest bear

       He shivers,
cradling the wine jug, his heart beating strangely;
his mind fills up with darkness

       overland, the inching caravans
       the blacked-out troop trains
       convoys through ruined villages
       along the Mekong

       merging
with the hydrocarbon-dark, headlight-inflamed Potomac

the little lights   the candles
flickering on Christmas eve
the one light left burning
in a front hallway   kerosene-
lit windows in the pitch dark
of back-country roads

                        His mind
plunges like a derrick
into that pitch dark as he uncorks the wine jug
and with a quick gesture not unlike
a signing with the cross (but he is a Quaker)
begins the anointing of himself with its contents,
with the ostensible domestic Rhine wine
or chablis, which is not wine—which
in fact is gasoline.

    tallow, rushlight, whale oil, coal oil,
    gas jet: black fat of the Ur-tortoise
    siphoned from stone, a shale-tissued
    carapace: hydrocarbon unearthed
    and peeled away, process by process,
    in stages not unlike the stages
    of revelation, to a gaseous plume
    that burns like a bush, a perpetual
    dahlia of incandescence, midway
    between Wilmington and Philadelphia

gaslight, and now these filamented
avenues, wastelands and windrows
of illumination, gargoyles,
gasconades, buffooneries of neon,
stockpiled incendiary pineapples,
pomegranates of jellied gasoline
that run along the ground, that cling
in a blazing second skin
to the skins of children

Anointing the overcoat, and underneath it the pullover
with one elbow out, he sees, below the whiplash threshold,
darkness boil up, a vatful of sludge, a tar pit,
a motive force that is all noise: jet engines,
rush-hour aggressions, blast furnaces,
headline-grabbing self-importances

the urge to engineer events
compel a change of government,
a change of heart, a shift
in the wind's direction—lust
after mastery, manipulations
of the merely political

Hermaphrodite of pity and violence, the chambered
pistil and the sword-bearing archangel,
scapegoat and self-appointed avenger, contend,
embrace, are one. He strikes the match.

A tiger leap, a singing envelope goes up,
blue-wicked, a saffron overcoat of burning

> *in the forests of the night*
> *make me thy lyre*

Evolving
out of passionless dismemberment,
a nerveless parturition, green wheels'
meshed intercalibration with the sun

A random leaf, seized by the updraft, shrivels
unresisting; fragments of black ash
drift toward the dahlia gardens

from dim tropisms of avoidance,
articulated, node upon internode,
into a scream, the unseen filament
that never ends, that runs
through all our chronicles

a manifesto flowering like a dahlia
into whole gardens of astonishment—
the sumptuous crimson,
heart's dark, the piebald
saffron and scarlet riding
the dahlia gardens of
the lake of Xochimilco:

Benares, marigold-garlanded
suttee, the burning ghats

alongside the Ganges: at
the An Quang pagoda, saffron
robes charring in fiery
transparency, a bath of burning

Scraps of charred paper, another kind of foliage,
drift toward the dahlia gardens

                              a leaf

              thou mightest bear

                        The extravaganza
of a man afire having seized, tigerlike, the attention
it now holds with the tenacity of napalm, of the homebound
file clerks, secretaries, minor and major bureaucrats,
superimposing upon multiple adjustments,
the fine tuning of Precaution and Accumulation,
the demands of Magnitude, what the concentric
groves of those archives have no vocabulary
for dwelling on, the uniformed man of action,
in whom precaution and the unerring impulse
are one, springs forward to pound and pummel,
extinguishing the manifesto as decently as possible.
                                        Someone,
by now, has sent for an ambulance.

The headlights crawl, slowed by increasing density,
along the Potomac, along the diagonal thoroughfares,
along the freeways, toward Baltimore, toward Richmond,
toward Dulles and toward Friendship Airport, the airborne
engines' alternating red

and green, a pause and then again a red,
a green, a waking fantasy upborne
on a lagoon of hydrocarbon, as
the dahlia gardens ride the lake of Xochimilco.
While the voiceless processes of a system
that in the end perhaps will have
refused nothing tangible, continue neither
to own nor altogether to refuse the burning filament
that runs through all our chronicles, uniting
system with system into one terrible mandala,
the stripped hydrocarbon
burns like a bush, a gaseous plume
midway between Wilmington and Philadelphia.

THE BURNING CHILD

After a few hours' sleep, the father had a dream
that his child was standing beside his bed,
caught him by the arm and whispered reproach-
fully: "Father, don't you see I'm burning?"
          —FREUD, *The Interpretation of Dreams*

Dreamwork, the mnemonic flicker
of the wave of lost particulars—
whose dream, whose child, where, when, all lost
except the singed reprieve, its fossil ardor
burnished to a paradigm of grief,
half a century before the cattle cars,
the shunted parceling—*links, rechts*—
in a blaspheming parody of judgment
by the Lord of burning: the bush, the lava flow,
the chariot, the pillar. What is, even so,
whatever breathes but a reprieve, a risk,
a catwalk stroll between the tinder
and the nurture whose embrace is drowning?

The dream redacted cannot sleep; it whimpers
so relentlessly of lost particulars, I can't
help thinking of the dreamer as your father,
sent for by the doctors the night he said the *Sh'ma*
over the dim phoenix-nest of scars
you were, survivor
pulled from behind a blazing gas tank

that summer on the Cape, those many years
before we two, by a shuttlecock-and-battle-
dore-, a dreamworklike accretion of nitwit
trouvées, were cozened into finding how
minute particulars might build themselves
into a house that almost looks substantial:
just as I think of how, years earlier,
the waves at Surfside on Nantucket, curveting
like herded colts, subsiding, turned
against my staggering thighs, a manacle
of iron cold I had to be pulled out of. Drowning,
since, has seemed a native region's ocean,
that anxiety whose further shores are lurid
with recurrences of burning.

The people herded from the cattle cars
first into barracks, then to killing chambers,
stripped of clothes, of names, of chattels—all those
of whom there would remain so few particulars:
I think of them, I think of how your mother's
people made the journey, and of how

                              unlike
    my own forebears who made the journey,
    when the rush was on, aboard a crowded
    train from Iowa to California, where,
    hedged by the Pacific's lunging barricades,
    they brought into the world the infant

who would one day be my father, and
(or the entire astonishment, for me, of
having lived until this moment would
have drowned unborn, unburied without
ever having heard of Surfside) chose
to return, were free to stay or go
back home, go anywhere at all—
                              not one
outlived the trip whose terminus was burning.

The catwalk shadows of the cave, the whimper
of the burning child, the trapped
reprieve of nightmare between the
tinder and the nurture whose
embrace is drowning.

NOTES

"The Outer Bar"

An expedition to a bar island off the coast of Maine, as recalled in midwinter, is the occasion and the subject here. Of the particular island Louise Dickinson Rich wrote in *The Peninsula* (Chatham-Viking, 1958, 1971, p. 153): "When there's an unusually low run of tide it's possible to get over there by walking across the exposed sand bar to Inner Bar Island and then scrambling ankle-deep along a rocky reef to Outer Bar. But you can't stay very long. The minute the tide turns you have to start back. If you wait too long you're going to be stuck out there for twelve hours, or until the next low tide; that is, unless you can attract the attention of a passing lobsterman who will take you off." Natural processes have lately made getting there a little easier, but not very much.

". . . fall, gall and gash the daylight": this phrase for the breaking surf derives, of course, from "The Windhover" by Gerard Manley Hopkins.

"Sea Mouse"

At the time of my sole encounter with the sea mouse—a glimpse of a swimming creature in a rock pool at low tide—I had no idea what in the world it could be. It was quickly identified by means of a pocket guide to seashore life. According to the *Columbia Encyclopedia,* it is a "marine worm of the genus *Aphrodite* with a short, broad, segmented body, found in moderately deep water. . . . The entire dorsal surface . . . is covered by long, feltlike threads called setae, which produce a brilliant iridescence. . . . Sea mice commonly reach 6 to 8 inches in length and 2 inches in width. They are classified in the phylum Annelida, class Polychaeta, family Aphroditidae."

"The Sun Underfoot Among the Sundews"

SUNDEW. Any of several insectivorous plants of the genus *Drosera,* growing in wet ground and having leaves covered with sticky hairs.

—*American Heritage Dictionary*

"Botanical Nomenclature"

Louise Rich on the seaside *Mertensia* (op. cit., p. 133): "For a long time nobody could tell me the name of what I consider the most beautiful wild flower I have ever seen anywhere. . . . Here it is known colloquially as 'that blue and pink flower that grows along the shore.' Everything about it is beautiful: the large, oval, silvery-green-gray leaves; the trumpet-shaped flowers which are pink when they open but turn to clear, pure blue within hours; and especially the habit of growth. The stems lie along the ground, radiating from a central taproot so symmetrically that the plant is a perfect disk, sometimes as much as four feet in diameter. The stems bear leaves along their entire lengths and the blossoms grow in clusters at the tips." Year by year, the plant has become increasingly rare in the places where I first encountered it.

"A Procession at Candlemas"

Fernand Braudel, *The Mediterranean and the Mediterranean World in the Age of Philip II,* Vol. I, translated by Siân Reynolds (Harper & Row, 1972, pp. 87, 88): "Transhumance . . . is simply one form of the Mediterranean pastoral way of life, alternating between the grazing lands of the plains and the mountain pastures. . . . Nomadism, on the contrary, involves the whole community and moves it long distances. . . . Today nomadism . . . consists of the knot of about ten people who might be seen round a fire at nightfall in one of the outer suburbs of Beirut; or at harvest time in Algeria, a few camels, sheep and donkeys, two or three horses, some women dressed in red, and a few black goat-skin tents amidst the stubble . . ."

Candlemas, celebrated on February 2, is the Christian feast of the Purification of the Virgin and the Presentation of the Infant Jesus in the Temple.

Peter Levi, text of *The Greek World,* photographs by Eliot Porter (Dutton, 1980, p. 77): "Archaeologists have pieced together in some detail the progress of the building on the Acropolis and have identified more than seventy-five different hands on the carving of the sculptures that made up the frieze of the Parthenon. Beginning in the southwest corner of the temple, it represented one of the city's greatest ceremonies, the Panathenaic procession that every four years brought a new sacred robe, the peplos, to Athena. Altogether the carvings showed more than four hundred human figures and more than two hundred animals. Undoubtedly that procession did, in real life, wind past the Parthenon. But the priest and priestess who stand among the gods are the servants of the ancient, doll-like wooden image of Athena, whose sanctuary had always been on the spot where the Erechtheum now stands. And it was to that wooden image—rather than to the monumental figure of Athena, made of marble, gold, and ivory, that was the central feature of the completed Parthenon—that the new robe was offered." Similar wooden images were central to the worship of Artemis at Brauron, and of Hera at Argos and Samos.

"The Dakota"

The most telling lines of this elegy ("all / the lonely people . . . Pick up / the wedding rice, take out / the face left over from / the funeral nobody came to") are lifted almost bodily from "Eleanor Rigby," recorded by the Beatles in 1966.

The Dakota is the apartment house where John Lennon lived, and in whose entryway he was murdered on December 8, 1980.

"Times Square Water Music"

The Times Square subway station in New York City is, among other things, a transfer point between the Interborough Rapid Transit and the Brooklyn-Manhattan Transit lines—hence IR and BM T. The initials N, RR, and QB, on the other hand, refer to particular routes on the BMT line; so far as I know, they mean nothing in particular.

Spleenwort is a kind of fern, and ouzels and pipits are small birds, all associated with water.

II. AIRBORNE, EARTHBOUND

"The Kingfisher"

The design here might be thought of as an illuminated manuscript in which all the handwork happens to be verbal, or (perhaps more precisely) as a novel trying to work itself into a piece of cloisonné. Its subject is an episodic love affair that begins in England and is taken up again in New York City. Dylan Thomas died there, at St. Vincent's Hospital, in November, 1953.

The kingfisher described in the final stanza is the European species, *Alcedo atthis,* which is conspicuous for its iridescent blue-green plumage. It is associated with the story of Alcyon and Ceyx, whom, in Ovid's *Metamorphoses,* Zeus turned into a pair of birds, and with the idea of "halcyon days"—a period of calm seas, and of general peace and serenity.

"The Smaller Orchid"

The flower referred to is one identified as fragrant ladies'-tresses, *Spiranthes cernua var. odorata.* It is notable, according to *Summer & Fall*

Wildflowers of New England, by Marilyn J. Dwelley, for having "a strong vanilla fragrance."

From Marcel Proust, *Remembrance of Things Past,* translated by C. K. Scott Moncrieff (Random House, 1934, Vol. I, p. 169): "She found something 'quaint' . . . in her orchids, the cattleyas especially (these being, with the chrysanthemums, her favourite flowers). . . ."

"Beethoven, Opus III"

Beethoven's piano sonata no. 32, Opus 111 (the arabic numbers tend to be misread and even, unfortunately, misprinted as a Roman numeral III, which would make it an early rather than a late composition) is his last work in that form, dating to the early 1820s. It figures in Thomas Mann's *Dr. Faustus* (Knopf, 1948; Vintage Books edition pp. 53–56), in E. M. Forster's *A Room with a View* (Knopf, 1932, p. 54), and in Milan Kundera's *The Book of Laughter and Forgetting* (Knopf, 1981, p. 161). I was first exposed to it, so far as I know, at a recital by Norman Carey, to whom the poem is dedicated. The notes by Eric Blom to the recording by Artur Schnabel on the Seraphim label have added much to my own understanding of the music.

Putti: the stylized infant cherubs that appear to soar, plunge or hover in some Italian and Spanish paintings on Christian themes.

"Beethoven might declare the air / his domicile, the winds kin": in a letter to Count Brunswick dated February 13, 1814, Beethoven wrote: "As regards me, great heavens! my dominion is in the air; the tones whirl like the wind, and often there is a whirl in my soul." Quoted in *Beethoven: The Man and the Artist, as Revealed in His Own Words,* edited by Frederick Kersh and H. E. Krehbiel (Dover, 1964).

III. HEARTLAND

"The Quarry"

From *Iowa: A Guide to the Hawkeye State* (Hastings House, 1938): "In the limestone quarries at LeGrand, Marshall County, finely preserved starfishes and crinoids (stone lilies) can be found. The abundance of these fossils and their state of preservation have made the limestones of the Mississippian age here of international importance. . . . The collection of B. H. Beane, of LeGrand, is on display at the State Historical Building in Des Moines." The Iowa Guide is also the source of the story of Lyman Dillon and his hundred-mile furrow. The capitol building described here is the one at Des Moines. An earlier building, the Old Capitol at Iowa City, was built of native limestone, not imported marble.

"The Woodlot"

Again according to the Iowa Guide, the anonymous inventor of barbed wire was an Iowa farmer.

"Imago"

IMAGO. 1. An insect in its sexually mature adult stage after metamorphosis. 2. *Psychoanalysis*. An often idealized image of a person, usually a parent, formed in childhood and persisting into adulthood.
                                        —*American Heritage Dictionary*
      ". . . the lit pavilions / that seduced her, their tailed child . . .": the reference is to Hans Christian Andersen's tale of the Little Mermaid, whose yearning to leave the water and become a human biped was fulfilled, but at a price. For reasons I can only guess at, this story affected me more powerfully than anything else I read as a child. Recently I have connected it—however fancifully—with the seas that in past eons covered

the region where I grew up. From *Basin and Range,* by John McPhee
(Farrar, Straus & Giroux, 1981): "Ohio, Indiana, Illinois, and so forth,
the whole of what used to be called the Middle West, is shield rock covered with a sedimentary veneer that has never been metamorphosed, never
been ground into tectonic hash—sandstones, siltstones, limestones, dolo-
mites, flatter than the ground above them, the silent floors of departed
oceans, of epicratonic seas. Iowa. Nebraska."

PHEROMONES: From Lewis Thomas, *Lives of a Cell* (Viking, 1974,
pp. 17–18): "Most of the known pheromones are small, simple molecules,
active in extremely small concentrations. . . . The messages are urgent,
but they may arrive, for all we know, in a fragrance of ambiguity. 'At
home, 4 p.m. today,' says the female moth, and releases a brief explosion
of bombykol, a single molecule of which will tremble the hairs of any
male within miles and send him driving upwind in a confusion of
ardor."

"The Local Genius"

From Glenway Wescott, *Goodbye Wisconsin* (Harper & Row, 1928,
p. 38): " 'Ah yes, yes. That was the young man who didn't know where
he was born. I thought it very curious.' 'Now what made you think that,
father? He was born in the Middle West.' 'But that's just it! I asked
him, and that is precisely what he said—all he could tell me.' "

The Iowa Guide, yet again, supplied the name of William Voss, inventor of the washing machine.

IV. TRIPTYCH

"Palm Sunday"

"Sing, my tongue, the glorious battle" is from a processional hymn, the
Pange Lingua, for which the sixth-century priest Venantius Fortunatus

(later canonized) supplied the opening lines; it is still sung at church services on Palm Sunday.

"Good Friday"

George B. Schaller, *Serengeti: A Kingdom of Predators* (Knopf, 1972, p. ix): "Though by inheritance a vegetarian primate, man has been a predator, a killer of animals, for at least two million years. . . . It is no coincidence that visitors to the African parks watch not the impala and zebra, but the lion and leopard. Even in sleep these big cats convey a feeling of barely contained strength, an ever-present threat of death, which man the hunter finds satisfying, though the danger is vicarious from the safety of a car. Our dual past still haunts us. We hear a lion roar and the primate in us shivers; we see huge herds of game and the predator in us is delighted, as if our existence still depended on their presence."

This dual past is the recurring nightmare of Christendom—a theology of the meek somehow trapped into giving its sanction to warfare. Yet the theology remains persuasive because it takes suffering seriously. And so, for all its impassivity, does the Darwinian theory of natural selection, which for many nowadays has acquired an almost theological authority. My own uneasiness gave rise to this meditation on the subject.

Charles Darwin married Emma Wedgwood, of the noted pottery manufacturing family. Three of their ten children died at an early age.

Olduvai Gorge, at the edge of the Serengeti Plain, is the site of the discovery by Louis and Mary Leakey of many prehistoric tools as well as of the fossil remains of proto-human beings.

"Easter Morning"

"A stone at dawn": the reference is to the New Testament, as in Mark 16 : 2–4: "And very early in the morning of the first day of the week, they came unto the sepulchre at the rising of the sun. And they said among themselves, Who shall roll us away the stone from the door of the sepulchre? And when they looked, they saw that the stone was rolled away: for it was very great."

V. WATERSHEDS

"Marginal Employment"

The treasures of the Duc de Berry are described in some detail by Barbara Tuchman in *A Distant Mirror* (Ballantine Books, 1978, pp. 427–28).

Several phrases straight out of the two "Byzantium" poems of William Butler Yeats will be noted.

"Tepoztlán"

From the *New Larousse Encyclopedia of Mythology* (Prometheus Press, 1959): "Huitzilopochtli ('hummingbird of the South,' or 'He of the South'), the god of war, was worshipped in the temple of Tenochtitlán where numerous human sacrifices were made to him."

". . . unaware that in some quarters / the place was famous": it had been made so, in anthropological circles, by Robert Redfield in *Tepoztlán, A Mexican Village: A Study of Folk Life* (University of Chicago, 1930), and later by Oscar Lewis in *Life in a Mexican Village: Tepoztlán Restudied* (University of Illinois Press, 1951).

". . . or, in their / musical Nahuatl, of *Huehuetzintzin*, / the Old Ones": Nahuatl is one of the languages spoken in Mexico before the

Spanish conquest. Of the Old Ones, Gilbert Murray wrote in *Five Stages of Greek Religion* (Doubleday Anchor Books, 1955, p. 35): "You go to the Chthonian folk for guidance because they are themselves the Oldest of the Old Ones, and they know the real custom."

"Remembering Greece"

From *Face of North America*, by Peter Farb (Harper & Row, 1963, pp. 20–21): "The myriad offshore islands on the Maine coast are the summits of hills drowned by the advance of the ocean upon the land. . . . In preglacial times some of the islands that now loom out of the ocean, such as Monhegan, must have been mountains that soared above the plain. . . . One obvious cause of the submergence of the shoreline is the melt of the glaciers. . . . But the immense weight of the glaciers themselves probably accounted for the major part of the submergence. . . . The land has since rebounded somewhat, but it is still about 1200 feet lower than at the beginning of the glacial age."

Aeschylus, *Agamemnon*, translated by Richmond Lattimore (*Complete Greek Tragedies*, Vol. 1, Modern Library, p. 70):

> . . . My maidens there!
> Why this delay? Your task has been appointed you,
> to strew the ground before his feet with tapestries.
> Let there spring up into this house he never hoped
> to see, where Justice leads him in, a crimson path.

"Trasimene"

From Baedeker's Touring Guide to Italy, 1962: "Situated near the constantly varying watershed between the Arno and the Tiber, in the marshy Chiana depression, the turquoise-blue Lake Trasimene repre-

sents the last untapped survivor of the sub-Apennine basin-lakes. . . .
It is now fed by rainwater only, and is expected to dry up in the not
distant future."

"Rain at Bellagio"

The scheme may be clearer if this poem is thought of as a meditation
in the form of a travelogue: the narrator, just arrived in Italy, is met at
Naples by a friend who has been living with her father at a villa on
Lake Como, and who is about to join an order of contemplative nuns in
England.

Fernand Braudel, *The Mediterranean and the Mediterranean World
in the Age of Philip II*, Vol. I, translated by Siân Reynolds (Harper &
Row, 1972, pp. 74, 76): "Rice growing in Lombardy meant the en-
slavement under terrible conditions of workers who were unable to
voice any effective protest since they were not organized. Rice fields do
not require labour all the year round, but large numbers of casual
workers for a few weeks, at the times of sowing, transplanting, and
harvest. This kind of agriculture depends entirely on seasonal migration.
It hardly requires the landowner to be present except for paying wages
and overseeing the gangs at work. . . .

"The vast low-lying plain of the Sienese Maremma, a real fever trap,
is, like its neighbour the Tuscan Maremma, dotted with noblemen's
castles. . . . Most of the year the masters live in Siena, in the huge
town houses still standing today, palaces into which Bandello's lovers
find their way, with the ritual complicity of the servants. . . . [The]
dénouement would take place in secret in the old castle in the Maremma, far from the town gossip and family control. Isolated from the
world by fever and the sultry heat, what better place could there be
for putting to death, according to the custom of Italy and the century,
of an unfaithful wife—or one suspected of being so?"

VI. HYDROCARBON

"Or Consider Prometheus"

It was Daniel Gabriel, in a poetry workshop at The New School, who led me to Charles Olson's *Call Me Ishmael* (City Lights Books, 1947), as a book no American poet should fail to read. For this advice, along with much else, I here acknowledge my indebtedness.

"The smuggled gem / inside the weed stem": Prometheus is said to have carried fire down from Olympus inside the stalk of a giant fennel.

Whales, dolphins, and porpoises are all air-breathing mammals; even though they spend their entire lives in the water, they must rise to the surface periodically to replenish their supply of oxygen. It is presumed that they evolved from a land-dwelling ancestor, whose ancestor in turn was an ocean-dwelling fish. What prompted this return to a life in the oceans is a matter of speculation—and although volition has no place in any theory of evolution, strictly speaking, the notion of a Road Not Taken becomes almost irresistible when the habits of the ocean-dwelling mammals and those of the tree-dwelling, prehensile, visually oriented monkeys (whose habits our own so much resemble) are compared.

"The Dahlia Gardens"

An account of the self-immolation of a thirty-two-year-old Quaker, Norman Morrison, in front of the Pentagon in Washington appeared in *The New York Times* on November 3, 1965. Although his name has since been forgotten in the United States, in 1978 it was (according to an American visitor whose report I happened to hear) still remembered in Vietnam.

"Midway between Wilmington and Philadelphia": the refineries of

Marcus Hook, Pennsylvania, with their perpetual gas flares, will be familiar to anyone who has traveled through the region via Amtrak.

Charles Olson's observation that the first oil well had been drilled as recently as 1859 was what dramatized for me the transitoriness of an entire culture founded on the use of petroleum: people to whom I report this fact are almost invariably startled, as though it could not possibly be true.

"The Burning Child"

The account from which the epigraph is taken appears at the beginning of Chapter VII of *The Interpretation of Dreams*, "The Psychology of the Dream-Processes," and is quoted here from the translation by James Strachey (Avon, 1965, pp. 547–48).

Amy Clampitt was born and brought up in New Providence, Iowa, graduated from Grinnell College, and from that time on lived mainly in New York City. Her first full-length collection, *The Kingfisher*, published in 1983, was followed in 1985 by *What the Light Was Like*, in 1987 by *Archaic Figure*, and in 1990 by *Westward. A Silence Opens*, her last book, appeared in 1994.

The recipient in 1982 of a Guggenheim Fellowship, and in 1984 of the fellowship award of the Academy of American Poets, she was made a MacArthur Prize Fellow in 1992. She was a member of the American Academy of Arts and Letters and was a Writer in Residence at the College of William and Mary, Visiting Writer at Amherst College, and Grace Hazard Conkling Visiting Writer at Smith College.

She died in September 1994.

A NOTE ON THE TYPE

This book was set on the Linotype in Granjon, a type named
after Robert Granjon. George W. Jones based his designs for
this type upon that used by Claude Garamond (c. 1480–1561)
in his beautiful French books. Granjon more closely resembles
Garamond's own type than do the various modern types that
bear his name. Robert Granjon began his career as type cutter
in 1523 and was one of the first to practice the trade
of type founder apart from that of printer.

Composed by American-Stratford Graphic
Services, Inc., Brattleboro, Vermont.
Printed and bound by American Book—
Stratford Press, Saddle Brook, New Jersey

Typography by Joe Marc Freedman